Cordially Invited

A SEASONAL GUIDE TO HOSTING ANY OCCASION AND MAKING A MEMORY OUT OF EVERY DAY

ZOE SUGG

HODDER &
STOUGHTON

Cordially Invited

A SEASONAL GUIDE TO HOSTING ANY OCCASION
AND MAKING A MEMORY OUT OF EVERY DAY

ZOE SUGG

HODDER &
STOUGHTON

First published in Great Britain in 2018 by Hodder & Stoughton
An Hachette UK company

1

A CIP catalogue record for this title is available from the British Library

Hardback ISBN 9781473687776
eBook ISBN 9781473687769

Colour origination by BORN
Printed and bound in Germany by Mohn Media

Hodder & Stoughton policy is to use papers that are natural, renewable and recyclable products and made from wood grown in sustainable forests. The logging and manufacturing processes are expected to conform to the environmental regulations of the country of origin.

Publisher: Briony Gowlett
Project Editor: Laura Herring
Art Director: Alasdair Oliver
Photographer: Susan Bell
Prop Stylist: Louie Waller
Food Stylist: Frankie Unsworth
Recipe Developer: Alexandra Heaton
Design: Helen Crawford-White of Studio Helen with Saffron Stocker
Senior Production Controller: Susan Spratt

With thanks to Daniel Cope for picture (middle row, right hand side) on page 80.
Additional photography and personal images supplied by the author.

The publisher would like to thank Lights4fun, Paperchase, Anthropologie, Peach Blossom, Talking Tables, Funky Monkey Tents and florist Yoko Edgeller for their kind supply of props.

This book contains references to drinking alcohol, the author and publisher encourages responsible drinking for those over 18 years old only.

Hodder & Stoughton Ltd
Carmelite House
50 Victoria Embankment
London EC4Y 0DZ

www.hodder.co.uk

INTRODUCTION

Ever since I can remember, home comforts have always been something of huge importance to me. I was that person in school who never wanted to stay over at people's houses for sleepovers, and I would make up silly excuses so I could go home to sleep in my own bed, in my own bedroom, under my own roof. You could say I took home comforts a little too literally.

This became particularly evident when, as an adult and I had to stay in hotels every now and then (which should have been so exciting), I struggled with it. The pillows weren't the same, the bedding wasn't mine, there was no personalisation and it felt to me like a very sterile environment. But after a few times staying away I came to notice all the little things that did make me feel at home. Like the welcome letter, the curation of snacks, the bottles of water on the bedside table and the bubble bath. When I have friends or family to stay, I always want them to feel like they're home away from home. I never want them to experience that same feeling of being in an empty hotel room, far away from all their personal comforts.

When someone is hosting me and they get out the cosy blankets, the fairy lights, the fresh sheets and the special tea they know I like, it means so much. It makes me feel really valued when someone goes the extra mile, adding those thoughtful details to make me feel fuzzy, relaxed and comfortable. And so I make it my absolute duty to give that very same feeling back to anyone that visits my house or attends a shindig I've put on.

From a very early age, I was aware of how much effort my mum would put into our birthday parties or our handmade fancy-dress costumes. Another child might have had their fancy shop-bought Thunderbirds outfit, but I was wearing Mum's finest mermaid tail made of shiny fabric with bubble wrap sewn in, fake glittery hair made from tinsel and a hand-held mirror made from cardboard with hundreds of real shells stuck to the back. She would spend hours making our birthday cakes from scratch, following very intricate detailed cake designs (one of which was a bear's picnic, complete with multiple fondant icing bears and teeny bits of icing picnic food) and would throw Halloween parties for her friends where she'd cover the whole house in cobwebs and hang plastic bats from the ceiling with string. I was in awe of how magical she always made everything feel. You could say I got my hostess gene from her!

So when I was old enough to have input on parties or celebrations, I'd go the extra mile, too. Through the years I've found that it really is the little touches that make the most impact. When I moved out and got my own place, I fully got stuck in and realised how much I adored bringing all my ideas together to make a real difference to a guest's experience. Like writing your guest's name on a chalkboard to welcome them on their arrival; spraying their pillow with lavender-scented sleep spray; creating a homemade overnight kit with a miniature toothpaste and a tasty midnight snack; and remembering to get their favourite granola in for breakfast. Beyond just these little touches I was coming into my own when it came to hosting friends and family. I'm a people pleaser through and through, but I'm also hugely creative and love having a project (I'm starting to think my career should have been in party planning). Nothing brings me more joy than putting together an ensemble of creative, fun elements to celebrate something... for someone else. I truly feel that having someone throw you a party is up there with one of the best feelings in the world, but throwing the party for someone else and seeing their face light up is even beyond that!

Hosting doesn't just mean being the queen of party planning though, it lies in how your guest feels when they're in your home – and what I hope this book will show is that it's the considered things like a fresh bunch of tulips on the nightstand and a spare phone charger (because you know they will have forgotten theirs) that makes a person feel truly welcome. *Cordially Invited* is a compilation of everything I've picked up and learned about being a good hostess – all the tips, tricks and inspiration that I'd like to share with you, whether it's a huge surprise birthday bash for your bestie, hosting friends in your home for the weekend or even a party for your dog.

Whether you're creative like my mum and me, or you struggle to assemble a paper lantern, I'm going to share some great ways to add a little something extra. I hope within these pages you'll find ideas for across the whole year, whether it's homemade decorations or seasonal baking or tips on how to decorate for any occasion and ways to spend time with friends outside. I want this book to be a source of inspiration. You don't have to be an absolute master chef in the kitchen either, if anything, that's probably my main weakness when it comes to hosting. For my mum, however, this is one of her favourite aspects of hosting guests (maybe one day I'll serve an eight-course meal good enough for a Disney banquet). But hopefully this book proves to you that you don't always need to spend days in the kitchen preparing a feast to bring a celebration to life. Whether you have all the time in the world, or none at all, whether you want to push the boat out or do things on a shoestring there will be something in here for you to ensure your guests have the perfect stay or talk about the party you planned them for years to come.

I hereby cordially invite you to join me through the seasons as I share my ideas for everything you might need in your back pocket in order to be the *hostess-with-the-mostess*.

Spr

ing

The saying 'spring has sprung' is always a lovely way to describe the start of this season. Everything seems to awaken after the long winter months in a very uplifting and beautiful way. Spring is home to the best floral bouquets and some of my most favourite flowers, including tulips in every shade, sunny daffodils and hyacinths, with their amazing scent which completely captures the season for me. It is a smell that brings absolute joy and breaks any of that winter gloom that can sometimes creep over you in January and February after all the Christmas and New Year frivolity has ended.

Trips to the garden centre suddenly become much more exciting (that's if, like me, you have an inner 70-year-old who has a great time in a garden centre!) and there are rows and rows of bulbs, seedlings and pretty flowers bursting up through the soil everywhere you look. At this time of year, I spend far too long in the seed aisle staring at all the tiny packets contemplating starting my own vegetable patch. I never actually follow through with it, but it's fun nonetheless. It's nice to wander around the garden centre as I'm often reminded of things I never thought I needed, like shears and garden twine, but you'll mostly find me in the house plants section filling my trolley with yet more greenery to distribute around my home. I won't be happy until my house resembles a jungle; I'd say I'm about half way there.

> Everything seems to awaken after the long winter months in a very uplifting and beautiful way.

My home - now a little more de-cluttered after a thorough post-Christmas spring clean - will be filled with glass jars of spring flowers, and I start to switch out heavier, warmer candle scents for much fresher, uplifting ones like 'tomato leaf' and 'wild mint'. Some people may think that candles are just for burning through the winter but I love to have some burning in spring to add a cosy glow when the weather is still a bit on the chilly side.

I used to shrug at the term 'spring cleaning' and didn't ever see the appeal of having a specific time of the year where you have a good old sort out through all those drawers and cupboards that you usually just throw things in randomly, locking the door and hoping for the best. As I'm getting older, though, spring is generally the time of year where I get the urge to clean. The spring months

always feel like a start of the year for me and I get a real boost of motivation and the feeling of new beginnings. What better task to tackle when you're in this mood than the drawer of 'stuff' and the corner in your wardrobe you refuse to look at?! You always feel so much better having done it, and it feels as though you are heading into the rest of the year in the best way possible, with everything in its place (for the time being, anyway...).

The weather is getting a bit warmer and the idea of going on long walks, and maybe even finding a perfect picnic spot that isn't a boggy mess is finally possible. With the birds singing, lambs in the fields and the sun a little higher in the sky, it's the time of the year that you can finally get your trainers on and enjoy more time outside. This is also made more possible by that extra bit of sunlight making the days that little bit longer (hallelujah). I also appreciate taking my dog Nala on a long walk without having to scrub a thick layer of mud off her paws when we get home! This not only saves me a bit of extra time to enjoy the evening but also allows her to be in fewer wet-doggy moods.

It's the time of the year that you can finally get your trainers on and enjoy more time outside.

Springtime is when everyone starts to come out of their winter hibernation and become a little more spontaneous with their social plans. Walks along the beach, late-night shopping and, if the evening is nice, a drink in a beer garden. It's like a practice run-up to summer, with a few extra layers!

Two big events in this season are my birthday and Easter – both very chocolate-heavy occasions that I really enjoy planning and celebrating in all their (usually) pastel glory! It's the perfect excuse to get back to baking lots of delicious sugary confectionery, and you can bet there will be some form of cupcake or an over-the-top three-tier cake on a glass cake stand in my kitchen. You're also more than likely to find me in the kitchen making up a batch of melted Easter egg chocolate and Shredded Wheat 'goodness' to snack on, maybe while watching a movie. This is meant to be made into Easter chocolate nests (see page 29), but I don't ever seem to get that far, as eating it warm from the bowl with a spoon is just too good to resist! In short, spring is simply wonderful!

SPRING TO-DO LIST

○ Have a good spring clean.

○ Switch up your bedding (to a lower-tog duvet).

○ Buy some new house plants.

○ Re-stock the pantry for spontaneous baking – check out the Easter baking recipes on pages 20–31.

○ Fill your home with floral bouquets – there are some tips on page 35.

○ Make pancakes (see the pancake recipe on page 20).

○ Visit the local garden centre for ultimate spring vibes.

○ Get out and scrub up the garden furniture and get creative with your outside space.

○ Discover new walks – locate the nearest bluebell wood (see page 46).

○ Go on the hunt for some new spring recipes.

○ Take endless photos of the cherry blossom on April walks.

○ Make some Easter decorations (see page 23).

○ Fly a kite (or attempt to).

○ Find the nearest farmers' market and enjoy the new-season veg.

○ Open the windows and doors to let in the fresh spring air (especially on a spring cleaning day).

○ Put on a raincoat, wellies, grab the cutest umbrella and embrace the spring showers and rainbows!

○ Throw an Easter egg hunt, followed by a big Sunday lunch (see pages 39–43).

○ Treat yourself to an Easter egg.

EASTER

Easter is one of the first seasonal events of the year that I get fully into. It's definitely one worth decorating the house for as it also marks the beginning of spring. Garden centres always have such lovely decorations, which don't tend to be very expensive, but they are also fairly easy to make yourself. I like to bring in some springtime branches and decorate them with Easter biscuits hung up on pretty ribbons (see page 26). I always have loads of bowls of mini pastel eggs around the house, I love a bit of Easter bunting too! (Check out the cute Easter bunny bunting on page 32.)

Growing up, Easter was always a really fun celebration. We'd craft Easter bonnets, make our own Easter eggs and eat more chocolate during those few days than any other time during the rest of the year. I have such lovely memories of my best friend and I at primary school, performing the Easter service to the parents, while wearing our extravagant straw hats complete with tiny fluffy chicks and colourful plastic eggs, not forgetting the fluffy bunny under each arm! We'd sing songs and read poems about spring and Easter and then look forward to the Easter holidays when we'd get Easter eggs, go and watch the lambing at the local farm and do an Easter egg hunt.

One thing you will notice throughout this book is that I love keeping up traditions. If something made you incredibly happy and brought you so many amazing memories as a child, then there's no reason why you can't bring elements of that into your adult life or pass those traditions on. If it brought you that much joy, it will no doubt bring others joy, too.

With this in mind, each year, around Easter time, I like to plan something fun with family. Being an adult, I think it's about adding a few little twists and bringing a few unexpected elements into the celebrations. We like to do a 'secret egg giving', where we pull names out of a hat and that person then buys one Easter gift for one other person – like an Easter secret Santa! (The Secret Bunny, if you like.) This allows you to get a little more creative with your gift, and also stops people from piling up mountains of chocolate that they have to get through.

Last year, I received a beautiful Easter display in a wooden trough, complete with tiny painted eggs and spring flowers. Nestled in amongst it were lots of my favourite chocolate bar (a Wispa, for those wondering!). It was a lovely spin on a traditional Easter egg.

We also like to play Easter games, and have even been known to do an Easter quiz in teams! And then afterwards, we gather round the table for a big Easter lunch.

Of course, the Easter season begins with one of my other favourite days of the year – pancake day! Shrove Tuesday is a lovely way to really mark the beginning of spring and I often have a few people over for a relaxed pancake-making party. You can go as wild as you want with the toppings and have a pancake flipping contest.

During these spring months, there are so many cute snacks and cakes to create with all the mini eggs and other chocolatey treats adorning the shelves in the supermarkets. Some of my absolute favourites include chocolate Easter egg nests (see page 29), Creme Egg brownies, marshmallow and Rice Krispie cakes and pretty much just any chocolate-filled cakes and cupcakes! I really find I get my bake on at this time of year, and it makes me (and my tummy) so happy.

EASTER TO-DO LIST

◯ Set up a secret Easter egg exchange with friends or family, allowing two weeks to buy or get creative.

◯ Make some cute Easter decorations (see page 23).

◯ Paint eggs.

◯ Make Easter-themed treats and snacks.

◯ Visit a lambing farm.

◯ Place tiny fluffy plastic chicks wherever you can around your home.

◯ Buy Easter eggs for an egg hunt (make sure to get different sizes and different colours if you're going to use a slightly more complex pointing system, see page 38).

◯ Prepare a roast dinner or offer to bring a part of the meal if you're visiting someone else. Maybe you could bring dessert, or a side dish? (see page 39 for my alternative Easter lunch recipe).

◯ Write up an Easter quiz if you're planning on having multiple teams and want to get a bit competitive.

◯ Create an Easter basket and deliver it to your friends or favourite neighbours.

◯ Eat lots of hot cross buns.

AMERICAN PANCAKES

I know crêpes are traditional on pancake day, but I love making fluffy American-style pancakes instead! I've definitely been known to pile mine up and cover them in chocolate chips, chocolate sauce and sprinkles – but here is a fresher, healthier option for celebrating one of my most favourite days of the year.

PREP: 5 minutes
COOKING: 20 minutes

MAKES about 10

200g plain flour
2 tsp baking powder
a pinch of salt
1 tbsp caster sugar
2 large eggs
250ml milk
1–2 tbsp vegetable oil,
  for frying

to serve
Greek-style yoghurt
sliced bananas and fresh
  berries (blueberries,
  raspberries and
  strawberries are
  my favourites)
honey
fresh mint
a sprinkling of icing sugar
  if you have a particularly
  sweet tooth (it makes
  them look pretty too)

Combine the dry ingredients in a large mixing bowl, then make a well in the centre. In a separate bowl or large jug, gently whisk the eggs into the milk, then pour this into your dry ingredients. Mix carefully with a spoon until just combined; small lumps are ok – you don't want to overmix it.

Heat a large, flat frying pan over a medium–high heat and add ½ tablespoon of vegetable oil. Use a piece of kitchen paper to rub the oil around the pan, then use a ladle to spoon some of your batter into the centre of the pan, into a pancake about 12cm in diameter.

Allow the pancake to cook – don't be tempted to flip too soon! Wait for small holes and bubbles to appear on the surface and it looks a little dry on top, about 2–4 minutes. Use a spatula to flip the pancake over and allow the other side to cook for 2 minutes more – it should be golden brown on both sides.

Put the cooked pancake on a heatproof serving plate in a low oven while you continue cooking the rest, stacking them onto the plate in the oven as you go. Swipe the oil-soaked kitchen paper around your pan before each new pancake, using a little more oil if it seems too dry.

Serve with dollops of yoghurt, some berries and a drizzle of honey. Garnish with fresh mint for a green flourish, and dust with icing sugar for the perfect finish.

EASTER DECORATIONS

Decorating at Easter allows you to play around with pastels and inject a slightly more whimsical style than you may usually prefer at other times of year. I love the lighter colours and fresh feel of spring decorations. Usually, I like to set up an Easter display in one area of my home and then have other little decorations elsewhere. When it comes to decorating, I think it's good to get creative and go a bit bigger than you might originally think you should! Think along the lines of Alice in Wonderland...

Over the years, companies and websites have started to fully embrace the Easter theme and each year it becomes easier to decorate at home. There is now such an expanse of choice and colour. You can find some great pieces at really accessible prices. There are also websites like Pinterest that are amazing if you want to get inspiration for your home, Easter table or chocolate treats – I could spend hours perusing online and believing afterwards that I really could create that giant Easter egg sculpture made of wicker!

Paper decorations are always a go-to for me. The fans are extremely easy to unfold and hang, but have a really great impact and don't cost a lot. I also love some springtime bunting. Paper pom pom bunting or honeycomb paper balls are beautiful, but I'm not going to lie – although I've seen people nail these in online tutorials I have never actually attempted them myself! But don't worry, I have some great – and slightly easier! – Easter bunny bunting on page 32. I love their cute little bunny tails. If you do fancy giving these or some paper decos a go, you could think about making it into a friends' night – get the snacks in and watch your favourite movies while making some pretty Easter decorations. It's a lovely low key way to catch up with people and you get something to keep at the end of the night. For a bigger event like a birthday or a wedding, I think having loads of paper decorations looks amazing, but for a smaller occasion, like Easter, you probably don't need quite so many.

I also like to bring a bit of nature into my Easter display, so I will often bring in a few stems or thin branches of blossom and put them in a big jug or vase. Then I'll decorate them with some pretty painted eggs or iced biscuits on ribbons – see my recipe for Easter biscuits on page 26. On the table, I'll then set out some delicious Easter treats for everyone to enjoy.

The decoration doesn't only apply to what you will have hanging up, but also to how you will display the dining table and the food for your Easter lunch. I like to tie in paper napkins to the colour theme, buy some paper straws for my Kilner-jar style glasses and maybe consider a table runner and sequin decorations to scatter on the table. One year I found a fake grass table runner, which proved to be perfect for the Easter table! Make sure you also include some fresh spring flowers in your setting. Spring has some of the prettiest and most divine smelling flowers and they look so cute and dainty displayed in little jam jars (see page 35 for how to make a perfect spring bouquet).

Easter is the perfect opportunity to give your home a touch of springtime magic after those long winter months, so enjoy the brighter colours and have fun! And don't forget the chocolate eggs...

DECORATIVE EASTER BISCUITS

This is my classic vanilla biscuit recipe – it's really reliable and perfect for decorating. The size of your cutters will determine how many biscuits you end up with but I like to have a range of different shapes for my Easter display. Don't forget to make holes in them if you want to hang them up with ribbons like I have.

PREP: 20 minutes
COOKING: 10–12 minutes
per batch
COOLING: 30 minutes

MAKES about 24,
depending on the size
of your cutters

1 egg yolk
250g butter, softened
140g icing sugar
2 tsp vanilla extract
375g plain flour, plus extra
for dusting

for the icing
225g icing sugar
1 egg white
gel food colouring of your
chosen colours (pinks,
purples, yellows and
greens are perfect)

essential equipment:
piping bags and nozzles (or
just snip a very small hole
at the end of your piping
bags)
biscuit cutters

Separate the egg yolk from the white and set aside the egg white for the icing later on. Using a spoon and a large bowl or in a stand mixer, mix together the butter, icing sugar, vanilla and egg yolk. Cream the mixture together until it's all mixed, then add in the flour a little bit at a time until it's all combined. Press the dough together into a ball, wrap in cling film and chill in the fridge for around 30 minutes.

Preheat the oven to 190°C/170°C fan/gas 5 and line a baking tray with non-stick baking paper.

You will need to bake the biscuits in batches. Dust some flour on your work surface and roll out half the dough using a floured rolling pin to about 5mm thick. Using a variety of cookie cutters in spring-like shapes (flowers, bunnies, eggs and chicks are fun), cut out biscuits and carefully place on the lined baking tray. If you'd like to make the biscuits into hanging Easter decorations, use a drinking straw to punch a hole into each biscuit, positioning the hole so that there is enough of a border around it so it can take the weight of the biscuit after decoration.

Pop the tray in the oven and bake for 10–12 minutes until lightly golden brown. Remove from the oven, leave to cool on the tray for a few minutes to firm up, then transfer to a wire rack. If the holes you've punched have closed over a little, use a skewer to enlarge them again while they're still warm. Allow to cool completely.

Add a new sheet of baking paper to the baking tray and repeat the rolling and baking with the second half of dough to make another batch. Gather together all your dough trimmings and roll these out too, to make extra biscuits.

While you're waiting for the biscuits to cool, make the icing. In a bowl, mix together the icing sugar with the egg white, adding a teaspoon or two of cold water if it feels too thick. Separate the icing into several small bowls and add a few drops of food colouring to each one. Stir vigorously to mix the colour through, and add more if you'd like it more vibrant.

Spoon the mixtures into separate piping bags fitted with thin nozzles or cut a very small hole at the end of your piping bag, and pipe onto the cooled biscuits. If you don't have multiple piping bags, you can use plastic sandwich bags with one corner snipped off – it works perfectly well!

You can also add sprinkles or whatever else you fancy for the perfect Easter display.

MILK CHOCOLATE NESTS

This is the chocolate mixture I was talking about on page 15 – most of the time it doesn't quite make it to the nest stage and I end up eating it straight from a bowl! If you do make it that far, they look really cute decorated with chocolate eggs – and maybe even a little fluffy Easter chick. They're a real childhood throwback for me!

PREP: 20 minutes
COOLING: 1 hour

MAKES 10

95g Shredded
  Wheat (4 large)
150g milk chocolate,
  broken into chunks
30-40 Mini Eggs,
  to decorate

essential equipment:
paper cupcake cases

Begin by setting out 10 pretty cupcake cases on a baking tray (or another tray that will fit into the fridge) and set to one side.

Using your hands, scrunch the Shredded Wheat in a bowl to break it up a little. You don't want crumbs, just to break up the larger chunks.

Put the milk chocolate in a heatproof bowl and set the bowl over a pan of barely simmering water, making sure the bottom of the bowl is not touching the water. Keep the heat low and stir gently as it melts. Once the mixture is smooth and melted, remove your bowl from the pan and turn off the heat.

Stir in the crushed Shredded Wheat and, using a metal spoon, gently fold the mixture to combine. The Shredded Wheat will break down a little more, which is fine. If the mixture begins to firm up while you stir, return the bowl to the pan of water and use the residual heat to loosen it up.

Spoon the mixture into the cupcake cases, roughly 2 tablespoons in each, and press down the centre of each one with the back of the spoon to create a nest shape. Place 3 or 4 Mini Eggs in each nest, before popping the lot into the fridge to set for an hour before serving. Once set, they will keep in an airtight container for a week.

PASTEL ICED ÉCLAIRS

These delicious cream-filled treats are perfect for your Easter display. You can actually make the éclair pastries a few days in advance. Keep them in an airtight container and fill them and ice them just before you'd like to serve them.

PREP: 20 minutes
COOKING: 30–35 minutes
DECORATING AND FILLING: 30 minutes

MAKES 12

for the choux pastry
100g plain flour
150ml water
50g unsalted butter, cut into cubes
2 tsp caster sugar
a pinch of salt
3 large eggs, beaten

for the Chantilly cream filling
25g icing sugar
200ml double cream

for the glaze
225g icing sugar
gel food colouring in purples and pinks

to decorate (optional)
edible flowers, sprinkles, sugar or edible gold leaf

essential equipment:
piping bags and a large (1.5cm) nozzle

Preheat the oven to 170°C/150°C fan/gas 3 ½ and line a baking tray with non-stick baking paper. Sift your flour onto a separate sheet of baking paper, so it's ready to quickly tip into the pan in one go.

Put the water, butter, sugar and salt into a medium saucepan over a high heat and, once it has just reached boiling point, remove from the heat and chute the flour into the pan in one quick movement. Using a wooden spoon, quickly beat the mixture until it is completely smooth, which takes some vigorous arm action!

Return the pan to a medium heat and cook your dough for just 1 minute, beating the mixture until it dries a little bit and clumps together, almost cleaning the sides of the pan. Remove from the heat again and gradually add in the eggs, beating all the time, until you have a smooth dough (be careful your mixture isn't too hot as this will create scrambled eggs! Not so yum). It will look strange and floppy for a while, but keep beating and it will come together. Spoon your warm dough into a large piping bag fitted with a large, 1.5-2cm, plain nozzle and let it cool and stiffen up a bit in the piping bag for about 5 minutes.

Using steady pressure, pipe 12 oblong shapes onto the lined tray to create 12 éclairs, each about 12cm long. Be sure to leave plenty of space around each one because they grow quite a lot in the oven. Pop into the oven and bake for 30-35 minutes or until golden.

Remove from the oven and leave to cool down. Once cooled, cut in half ready to fill with the cream.

To make the Chantilly cream filling, sift the icing sugar into the cream in a bowl and whisk until it forms soft peaks. Be careful not to overwhip it. Transfer the cream to a piping bag fitted with a thick nozzle, or cut a hole at the end of your piping bag. Gently pipe the cream along the bottom part of each éclair and place the top half over the cream.

Make the glaze by mixing the icing sugar with a little hot water, 1 teaspoon at a time, until you have a thick, spreadable consistency. If it does get too thin, add some more icing sugar. For different colours, divide the icing between small bowls and stir in 1-2 drops of gel food colouring. Place the cooled, filled éclairs on a wire rack and spoon the glaze over the top of each. Let the glaze set for 10-15 minutes before serving.

If you're feeling adventurous or particularly creative, you can add edible flowers, sprinkles, sugar or edible gold leaf to make them look even more adorable.

EASTER BUNNY BUNTING

This cute bunny bunting really completes an Easter display. Choose a colour to go with your theme – or go multicoloured pastel!

You will need:

sheet of card
sheets of coloured card
pencil
paper scissors
small pom pom maker
   or fork, and yarn
   (or shop-bought
   pom poms)
twine or ribbon to
   hang it up
hot glue gun, washi tape
   or double-sided sticky
   tape

TIP

For an extra touch you can paint the twine to match your colour theme.

Making the bunnies

1 Draw the outline of a bunny onto a sheet of plain card – there are some great free templates online. Cut around the outline to create your bunny template.

2 Using your card template, trace the bunny outline onto sheets of different coloured card. You will need 5 or 6 bunnies for each metre of bunting that you plan to make. Carefully cut around each traced bunny shape, cutting just inside any pencil markings so they won't show.

Making the pom poms

3 If you're like me and you prefer to buy your pom poms, then skip this part! Alternatively, if you're feeling a little more adventurous or own a pom pom maker, follow these steps... If using a pom pom maker, open up the maker at its hinge to separate the two halves. Wind yarn around the first curved half, before moving on to the second curved half – both halves of the pom pom maker should be completely full with yarn. When the two halves of the pom pom maker are full, close the maker and fasten the clasp. Using small, sharp scissors, insert the tip of the blades in the yarn and snip all the way round the

circumference of the pom pom maker. Take another length of yarn and wrap it around the cut centre line of the maker. Pull it tight and knot to secure the pom pom. Repeat this several times. Open up the pom pom maker and gently tease the pom pom off. Trim any straggly bits of yarn to ensure a neat round.

Alternatively... If using a fork, wrap the yarn around the two outer prongs of the fork until the fork is very full. Using a separate length of yarn, tightly tie the yarn on the fork in the centre between the middle prongs. Slide the wraps of yarn off the fork and cut the loops at each side to release the strands. Trim any straggly bits of yarn to ensure a neat round.

Assembling and hanging the bunting

4 Cut your twine or ribbon to the length you want your bunting to be. Using a hot glue gun, washi tape or sticky tape, fix the twine to the centre back of each bunny at intervals of roughly 20cm, varying the direction they face.

5 Using the hot glue gun or double-sided sticky tape, fix a pom pom tail onto each bunny.

6 Hang the bunting in place by tying the ends of the twine to a secure fixed point, or with washi tape on a clean wall surface.

FLOWER ARRANGING

Having beautiful blooms scattered around the house is the perfect way to bring the outside in and create a bit of elegance and colour during different times of the year. Spring for me is when a lot of my favourite flowers and bouquets are grown and arranged. I am a sucker for a hyacinth, as these smell absolutely incredible and I also love the very traditional daffodils and tulips around this time of year. You can buy an already made spring bunch, although it's quite nice to arrange your own in larger vases, jugs or little jars to put on windowsills, tables and mantelpieces too, and it's really not that difficult. The two things I think make the most difference to the longevity of your bouquets is to trim the ends before displaying them and to replace the water to keep them looking fresher for longer! There are some tips below on styling the bunch before displaying it, so you get the maximum floristry feel.

Choosing your flowers

If certain flowers are in season at the same time, then the chances are those colours will work together too. If you're unsure, stick to three or four classic spring shades, such as green, white and yellow, with a colourful splash of pink. To make flowers go further, add in some extra greenery or small twiggy branches – I also like to bring in a small blossoming branch to use in a display (see my Easter table on pages 24–25). Buy tulips and daffodils that are still in bud, rather than fully in flower. This way you can enjoy each stage of the bloom over a longer period. During spring, potted bulbs such as hyacinths, freesias and paperwhites are also very long-lasting, and reward with their cheering colours and amazing scent.

How to:

1   Measure your flower stems up against your chosen vase. A good rule of thumb is to make the stems twice the height of the vase. But if you are using a shorter round vase or jar, you might want to cut the stems so that the flower heads sit right on a level with the top of the jar to echo its round shape.

2   Snip the stems at a 45° angle (to help them absorb water) and remove any leaves or side shoots that will sit under the water line (so they don't go mouldy).

3   Hold one flower stem in your hand to start the posy. With your other hand, add more stems – a flower and a piece of foliage alternately. Hold the stems flat in the palm of your hand, using your thumb and forefinger to keep them in place. Keep turning the bouquet as you add the next stem. Adding each stem in a spiral movement keeps the bouquet in an even shape.

4   If you are putting your posy straight into a vase, add some plant food to the water before carefully placing your arrangement in the vase. Keep the vase topped up with water – flowers like tulips can be extremely thirsty.

5   If you are giving your posy as a gift, keep it in a vase of water until just before you are going to give it away. Then wrap it in simple brown paper or wrapping paper and tie with twine or raffia.

TIP

Make sure that the weight of the flowers won't topple over the vase. If you need to, add marbles to the vase to make sure your arrangement is stable. If you're using a glass vase, then lining the inside of the vase with moss is a lovely touch and will disguise any marbles.

PANTRY & KITCHEN SHELVES

One of things I have found the most useful in hosting parties or having people over is my ever-growing collection of kitchen and dinnerware which I store in my pantry and kitchen (and shove into every cupboard I can). I'm much more of a baker than I am a chef, so my bakeware is a little more impressive than anything else. I even have a drawer that is full of cupcake cases and sprinkles (definitely excessive, but undeniably my favourite drawer in the entire house). I am aware that most people who have a pantry use it for housing all their tins and long-lasting food such as pasta and rice, which I do have on the shelves, but I mostly like to keep things like cake stands, large serving dishes, jugs, teapots, champagne glasses and my everyday plates and bowls on display. I actually find styling these shelves really therapeutic as well as exceptionally helpful for having things you may need for hosting right there and easy to grab! I like to stack a few of my favourite recipe books on a shelf, and pop a few trailing plants on there too, as it brings it to life a little bit!

As I became an adult, I found that the items most likely to make it onto my birthday or Christmas lists were a nice gravy boat or a beautiful pie dish, and I know I'm not alone in this! When you move out into your own place or with other people, you soon come to realise just how much your parents had tucked away in all those cupboards that you never really had to think about. The whisks, mixers, baking tins, side plates, red wine glasses, white wine glasses (and yes, I've discovered the differences between the two), champagne flutes, napkin rings, teapots, milk jugs (and if you're anything like my mum, a jug in every size and every material possible), salad servers, rolling pins, scales, glass milk bottles... the list is endless.

I have been growing my collection of useful hosting equipment from around the age of 18. I still find it so exciting when I come across something that I think will be really handy, and I have found uses for absolutely everything I have gained over the years. Some of the best places to shop for unique home items, alongside the more obvious and modern places, are antique shops, charity shops or car boot sales! I picked up this tip from my mum, as I spent many a Sunday morning traipsing through fields with her in search of beautiful knick-knacks to bring home and put on her shelves. Antique and thrift shops have some of the most beautiful large silver serving spoons, jugs and vases and it's so much fun to upcycle things and give them purpose again, even if that purpose is not what they were intentionally made for!

These are the items I've got in my cupboards and on my shelves that I have found the most useful, and always advise people get if they have an inner hostess just waiting to be unleashed:

Small dishes and pinch pots. These are amazing to pop dips, sauces and nibbles in, and I find I use these more than anything else.

A large wooden cheeseboard or plank. I got this idea from Jamie Oliver's restaurants as they always serve the antipasti on one. I've used mine so much! It's so great to chuck food on, looks impressive and it's easy for everyone to help themselves. It also creates more of a centrepiece for the meal. I also love to use marble chopping boards and slabs of slate as platters to serve food on!

Kilner-jar-style glasses. I've used these for so many things, the obvious being lovely drinks but also desserts, flower arrangements and herb gardens (see page 108).

Mum's tip

Serve your food on unusual or different dishes – desserts in vintage teacups or pretty glasses are particularly lovely. Charity shops are a great place to pick up kitchenware in general if you are on a budget. Don't feel that everything has to match, sometimes it adds a lot more decoration and character to a table setting when things are very mismatched!

EASTER EGG HUNT

When you think of an Easter egg hunt, you may well imagine very young children scouting out little chocolate eggs with their cute baskets in a very well-behaved and slow-paced manner in the back garden. If you have children of your own or younger family members, this may be the version of an Easter egg hunt that you usually participate in. However, *this version* is definitely slightly different...

Imagine a group of adults all running around pushing each other out of the way after a couple of beverages collecting points with each different egg, sort of like an episode of *Finders Keepers*. It's so much fun! You either designate one 'egg planter' who can't participate in the finding, or you give each person a room and the same number of eggs. Each person then hides the eggs REALLY well in their room for the others to find. A good tip – learnt from experience! – is to take photos on your phone of where you've hidden all your eggs so you can remember where any unfound eggs are. On multiple occasions we've lost eggs and found them months later, half-melted into the furniture! Once the eggs are hidden, everyone gathers in the hallway and the countdown begins!

Everyone then scatters off in different directions hoping to grab the most eggs. You can only really play this if you have a very competitive family or some equally eager friends, otherwise I can't imagine it will have quite the same thrill. We assign different eggs different numbers of points (yes, we take it very seriously). Larger eggs will have fewer points, 'rare' eggs will have more points and smaller eggs will be like hitting the jackpot. You can also add decoy eggs that don't count for anything. Once all the eggs have been found, you tally up the points of each person's collected eggs and the winner gets a prize, usually a fancy chocolate egg. It's a lot of fun, and it also means keeping up a childhood tradition that you may not have done in a while.

You can also get a bit more crafty with this if there is a larger group of you – maybe ask people to wear bunny ears, funny masks or even go as far as giving each person a bunny costume they have to hop around in. (I should imagine this is very dependent on how much alcohol you'd usually consume on this day or the types of people you're playing with – you might not want your grandad hopping about the garden!)

Afterwards, once everyone has worked up a bit of an appetite running around the place, it's time to gather around the table to enjoy a big Easter Sunday lunch. Then it's to the sofa to eat A LOT of chocolate...

> On multiple occasions we've lost eggs and found them months later, half-melted into the furniture!

TIP

Have some pretty grab bags to hand so any leftover Easter snacks can be distributed among your guests or taken into work to share with colleagues. I don't know about you, but whenever I bake, I definitely over-bake. There's no way my boyfriend and I will consume all of those éclairs (see page 30) or double chocolate and Creme Egg cupcakes over the course of three days! Sharing is caring, after all.

A TWIST ON SUNDAY LUNCH

Instead of a traditional roast next Sunday, why not try this Moroccan-style feast for an injection of spring? The chicken is cooked with pomegranate molasses and preserved lemons, and it's served with spiced potatoes, a really fresh-tasting broad bean salad, and some grilled asparagus with tahini. See overleaf for photograph.

MOROCCAN-STYLE POMEGRANATE CHICKEN WITH SPRING SIDES

PREP: 10 minutes
COOKING: 70–80 minutes

SERVES 6

2 small preserved lemons
5 garlic cloves, peeled
4 sprigs of rosemary, leaves only
2 tsp coarse sea salt
2 tsp freshly ground black pepper
4 tbsp olive oil
5 tbsp pomegranate molasses
3 red onions, peeled and cut into chunky wedges
2 chickens, 1–1.5kg each (this gives you enough for leftovers)
150ml water
100g pomegranate seeds, to serve
a handful of mint leaves, to serve

Preheat the oven to 180°C/160°C fan/gas 4.

Finely chop the preserved lemons with the garlic and rosemary, then transfer to a pestle and mortar with the salt and pepper. Grind the ingredients together to a coarse paste, then add 2 tablespoons of the olive oil and your pomegranate molasses and mix to combine using a small spoon. Set to one side.

Scatter the red onion wedges into a large roasting tin big enough to fit the chickens side by side – if you don't have one big enough, you can use two and divide the onions evenly between them. Drizzle the onions with the remaining 2 tablespoons of olive oil.

Use clean hands to slather the chickens, inside and out, with the lemony paste, then place the chickens on top of the onions in the roasting tin. Pour the water into the tin, avoiding pouring it over the chicken. Cover the tin loosely with tin foil, pop in the preheated oven and cook for 40 minutes, then remove the foil and continue cooking for another 30 minutes, or until the chickens are fully cooked. To test, cut into the crease where the leg joins the breast – if the juices run clear, it's done.

Remove from the oven and allow to rest for a few minutes before transferring your chickens to a chopping board. Pull the meat away from the bones and shred it with two forks. Add the pulled meat back to the roasting tin and toss with the onions and roasting juices. Serve in the tin, or transfer to a serving platter before scattering the pomegranate seeds and mint leaves over the top.

side dishes continued on pages 42–43

Mum's tip

Put out snacks and nibbles to go alongside a drink as guests arrive. This gives them a chance to chat whilst you're preparing dinner and doesn't put as much pressure on you to hurry up and serve food as people won't be as hungry.

BROAD BEAN, PEA & FETA SALAD

PREP: 10 minutes
COOKING: 6 minutes

500g podded broad
  beans, fresh or frozen
250g frozen petits pois
200g feta, crumbled
finely grated zest of
  ½ lemon
10g fresh mint leaves,
  finely chopped
95g lamb's lettuce
80g pea shoots

for the dressing
2 tbsp honey
3 tbsp lemon juice
1 tbsp white wine vinegar
3 tbsp olive oil
salt and black pepper

Bring a large pan of water to the boil over a high heat.

Meanwhile, make your dressing by whisking the honey, lemon juice and vinegar together in a small bowl. Season with salt and pepper, then add the olive oil in a steady stream, whisking all the time to combine it well.

Once the water boils, tip in the broad beans. Cook for 3 minutes, then add the peas, bring back to the boil and cook for 3 more minutes. Drain the beans and peas into a colander, rinse under the cold tap for a few seconds then allow them to drain well and cool for a few minutes.

Put the crumbled feta into a large salad bowl and add the lemon zest and chopped mint. Give the beans and peas a final shake in the colander before tipping them into the bowl and stir with a big spoon to combine with the mint and feta. Pour over most of your dressing and toss again.

Add the lamb's lettuce and pea shoots just before serving and toss gently. Add a little more dressing if you think it needs it.

SMASHED ZA'ATAR SPICED POTATOES

PREP: 5 minutes
COOKING: 35 minutes

2kg small new potatoes
  (as small as possible),
  scrubbed
5 garlic cloves, unpeeled
3 tbsp olive oil, plus an
  extra 2 tsp to drizzle
4 tsp za'atar
salt and black pepper

Preheat the oven to 190°C/170°C fan/gas 5.

In a mixing bowl, toss the potatoes and garlic cloves in the olive oil and some salt and pepper, then tip into a baking tray in an even layer.

Pop the tray into the oven and bake for 25 minutes, then remove from the oven and, using a potato masher or large fork, press gently on each potato just to break the skin and flatten it a little. Drizzle with the 2 teaspoons of olive oil and scatter over the za'atar. Pop the tray back into oven on a high shelf for another 10 minutes to crisp everything up.

GRIDDLED ASPARAGUS
WITH TAHINI

PREP: 5 minutes
COOKING: 8–10
minutes

3 tbsp sesame seeds
2 bunches of asparagus,
   woody ends trimmed
2 tbsp olive oil

for the tahini dressing
4 tbsp tahini
juice of 1 lemon
1½ tbsp runny honey
1–2 tbsp warm water
3 tbsp olive oil
salt and black pepper

To toast your sesame seeds, preheat a dry frying pan over a medium–high heat. Add the seeds and toast gently for 5–6 minutes, tossing them in the pan until golden. Don't leave them unattended – they can turn from perfectly toasted to burnt in just a few seconds! Tip onto a plate and set to one side.

To make the dressing, in a small bowl, whisk the tahini with the lemon juice and honey. Add some warm water, a little at a time, to loosen the mixture, then add the olive oil, whisking all the time. Season with a pinch of salt and a few cracks of black pepper and set to one side while you prepare the asparagus.

Place the asparagus spears on a baking tray. Drizzle with the olive oil, sprinkle over a pinch of salt and some pepper and shake the tray back and forth to roll and coat the spears in a thin layer of oil.

Preheat a ridged griddle pan over a high heat and, when the pan is nice and hot, add the spears in a single layer. If you can, try to position them on the diagonal so they get nice, slanted grill marks. (If you don't have a griddle pan, you can use a regular frying pan but you won't get the charred lines.) Leave to cook for 2–3 minutes then use tongs to turn the spears individually, allowing them to cook on all sides. When they have nice, even grill marks and are slightly floppy, remove them to a serving plate or platter. (The asparagus can also be cooked in the same way on a barbecue.)

Whisk your dressing to loosen it a little before drizzling several big spoonfuls over the pile of asparagus. Sprinkle the sesame seeds over the top and bring to the table. You will probably have some extra dressing left over, so save it and keep it in the fridge – it's delicious on salads and cooked vegetables as well as with leftovers in a rice bowl (see page 44).

LEFTOVER RICE BOWLS

These bowls are a really versatile way of using up whatever odds and ends you have left over from the day before – you can always make some new extras if you don't have enough. Brown rice is a great starting point, but you can also use spelt, pearl barley or quinoa. Just check the packet for how much to cook for each serving, as these differ from grain to grain. To make these vegan, you can leave out the chicken and make the tahini dressing without honey.

PREP: 20 minutes
COOKING: 40 minutes

SERVES 3–4

125g brown rice (about 250g cooked weight) or another grain, such as barley, spelt or quinoa (see intro)
2 sweet potatoes, washed but unpeeled
1 red onion, peeled and cut into chunky wedges
40ml olive oil
3 tsp sweet smoked paprika
1/2 cauliflower, cut into florets
1 x 400g tin of chickpeas, drained and rinsed
1 tsp ground cumin
1/2 tsp dried oregano
1/2 tsp ground turmeric
100g kale, toughest stalks removed, leaves torn into large pieces
leftover cooked chicken, shredded (about 150g per person)
leftover griddled asparagus and other cooked veg (about 125g per person) from page 43
1 x quantity of Tahini dressing (see page 43)
mixed seeds, toasted for 30 seconds in a dry pan
salt and black pepper

Preheat the oven to 200°C/180°C fan/gas 6.

Cook your rice or grain according to the packet instructions, then drain well.

Cut the sweet potatoes in half lengthways, then into chunky half-moon slices, about 1.5cm thick. Put into a large mixing bowl with the onion wedges and drizzle with 1 tablespoon of the olive oil, 1 teaspoon of the smoked paprika and a generous pinch of salt and black pepper. Toss well to coat before tipping out onto a baking tray. Pop in the oven and roast for 15 minutes.

Meanwhile, put the cauliflower florets into the mixing bowl, add 1 teaspoon of the olive oil and toss to mix – the cauliflower will pick up a little of the seasoning left in the bowl. Remove your tray from the oven and scatter the cauliflower onto the tray over the top of the sweet potato and onion. Pop the tray back into the oven for another 10 minutes.

While the cauliflower is in the oven, heat a frying pan over medium–high heat and, when hot, add 1 tablespoon of the olive oil. Tip the drained chickpeas into the pan, followed by the remaining 2 teaspoons of smoked paprika, the cumin, oregano and turmeric. Stir with a spoon to coat the chickpeas in the spices, then allow them to cook for 8–10 minutes until crisp and fragrant. Remove from the heat and set aside.

Add the kale to your mixing bowl, drizzle with the remaining 1 teaspoon of oil and a pinch each of salt and pepper. Toss the kale to coat it, then remove the tray from the oven and spread the kale out over the top of the cauliflower before returning the whole thing to the oven for a final 4–6 minutes. The kale should crisp up around the edges, but not brown too much.

Divide your cooked rice or grain between three or four big bowls, then divide the roasted veg between them, spoon over the chickpeas and add your shredded chicken and any leftover cooked vegetables you have. Drizzle with a little dressing, scatter with a few toasted mixed seeds and tuck in!

TIP

You could use reheated leftover roast potatoes in place of the sweet potatoes, mixed roast vegetables in place of the cauliflower and reheated steamed vegetables instead of the kale. Also try the Roasted red peppers on page 52.

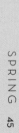

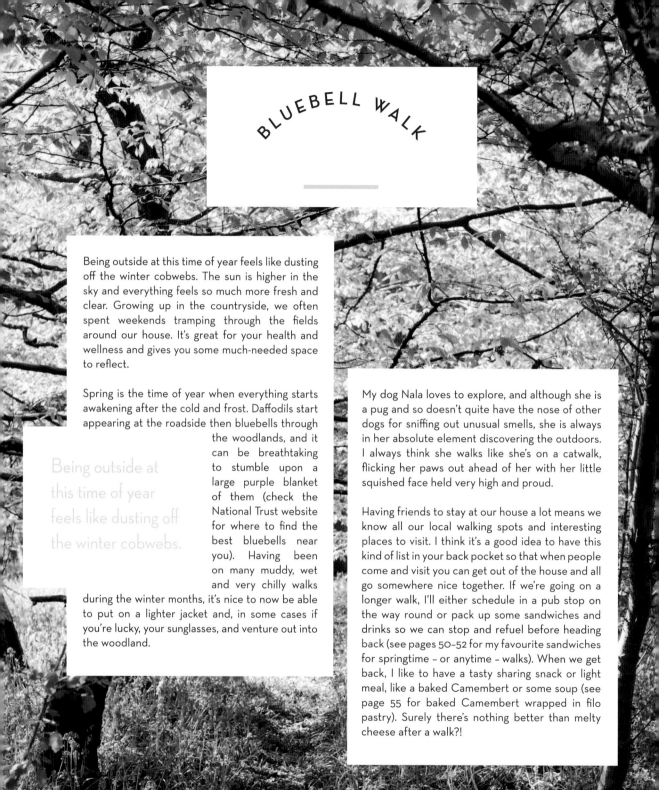

BLUEBELL WALK

Being outside at this time of year feels like dusting off the winter cobwebs. The sun is higher in the sky and everything feels so much more fresh and clear. Growing up in the countryside, we often spent weekends tramping through the fields around our house. It's great for your health and wellness and gives you some much-needed space to reflect.

Spring is the time of year when everything starts awakening after the cold and frost. Daffodils start appearing at the roadside then bluebells through the woodlands, and it can be breathtaking to stumble upon a large purple blanket of them (check the National Trust website for where to find the best bluebells near you). Having been on many muddy, wet and very chilly walks during the winter months, it's nice to now be able to put on a lighter jacket and, in some cases if you're lucky, your sunglasses, and venture out into the woodland.

Being outside at this time of year feels like dusting off the winter cobwebs.

My dog Nala loves to explore, and although she is a pug and so doesn't quite have the nose of other dogs for sniffing out unusual smells, she is always in her absolute element discovering the outdoors. I always think she walks like she's on a catwalk, flicking her paws out ahead of her with her little squished face held very high and proud.

Having friends to stay at our house a lot means we know all our local walking spots and interesting places to visit. I think it's a good idea to have this kind of list in your back pocket so that when people come and visit you can get out of the house and all go somewhere nice together. If we're going on a longer walk, I'll either schedule in a pub stop on the way round or pack up some sandwiches and drinks so we can stop and refuel before heading back (see pages 50–52 for my favourite sandwiches for springtime – or anytime – walks). When we get back, I like to have a tasty sharing snack or light meal, like a baked Camembert or some soup (see page 55 for baked Camembert wrapped in filo pastry). Surely there's nothing better than melty cheese after a walk?!

GETTING THE MOST OUT OF YOUR WALK

Camera: I love instant cameras at the moment as they are great for scrapbooking or for popping into glass frames to remember special moments.

Sandwiches and flasks of hot drinks: something that travels well and is fairly easy to eat (see pages 50–52 for some sandwich options). Good drinks to pack into a flask include hot chocolate or warm cranberry and apple juice.

Umbrella: the weather can be a little unpredictable at this time of year so it's best to be prepared.

Blanket: the ground may still be damp, but it's nice to be able to sit somewhere with a good view, for a break and something hot to drink.

Layer up: it's still a bit nippy in the air, as the sunshine can be a bit deceiving, and the first place I always feel the cold is my hands! Keep some spare socks and gloves (and blister packs) for guests.

PACK-UP SANDWICHES

These are great sandwich options for country walks (or if you're feeling hungry at home!). You can mix up the breads and fillings, but I think these combos work best. Wrap them up tightly and pack them in your bag with a flask of something warm to drink. See page 53 for photograph.

CORONATION CHICKEN

PREP: 5 minutes
MAKES 4

350–400g cooked chicken (ideally leftover from a roast)
2 spring onions, trimmed and thinly sliced
3 tbsp mayonnaise
2 tbsp Greek-style yoghurt
2 tbsp curry powder
1 tsp ground turmeric
1 tbsp mango chutney
1 tsp honey
finely grated zest of 1 lime
a pinch of cayenne pepper (optional)
salt and black pepper

to serve
1 ciabatta
Cos lettuce leaves
50g toasted flaked almonds

Chop the chicken into 2cm chunks and put into a mixing bowl with the spring onions, mayo, yoghurt, curry powder, turmeric, mango chutney, honey, lime zest and some salt and pepper to taste. Mix gently with a large metal spoon to coat the chicken in the dressing. Taste and adjust the seasoning, and if you'd like it a little spicier, add just a tiny pinch of cayenne pepper.

Slice the ciabatta in half lengthways and lay the two halves cut side up on your work surface. Layer the bottom half with some crisp Cos lettuce leaves and pile the chicken mixture on top. Sprinkle the flaked almonds over the top of the chicken and replace the top half of the ciabatta loaf. Press down gently and cut into four with a serrated knife.

TIP

To make this recipe vegetarian, replace the chicken with a 400g tin of rinsed and drained chickpeas, and to make it vegan, replace the mayo and Greek yoghurt with dairy-free yoghurt and leave out the honey.

HAM, CHEDDAR & CHUTNEY

PREP: 15 minutes
COOKING: 2–2½ hours
MAKES 4 (with leftover chutney)

for the chutney (makes enough to fill a 500g jar)
1 white onion, diced
3 Bramley apples (about 600g in total), peeled and cut into 1–1.5cm chunks
120g raisins
a pinch of salt
½ tsp dried chilli flakes
½ tsp yellow mustard seeds
1 tsp ground cinnamon
2 tsp grated fresh ginger
500ml cider vinegar
500g light muscovado sugar

for the sandwiches
8 slices of brown, seeded bread
butter, for spreading
2–3 tbsp chutney (see recipe above)
1–2 tsp English mustard (optional)
150g mature Cheddar, sliced
200g thinly sliced smoked ham
a handful of pea shoots (optional)

First make the chutney. Add all the ingredients to a large saucepan. Bring to the boil over a high heat, then reduce the heat to medium-low and allow to simmer for 2–2½ hours, stirring often with a wooden spoon. The mixture will reduce/thicken and darken, and you'll know it's done when you can scrape your spoon through the centre of the pan and see the bottom for a few seconds before the chutney settles again. Spoon your warm chutney into a sterilised (see below), warmed 500g clip-top jar, seal and allow to cool completely at room temperature before storing. Once opened, keep in the fridge.

When ready to assemble your sandwiches, lay your bread out on your work surface and butter each slice. Spread your chutney on 4 of the slices of bread and, if you like, spread the other 4 slices with mustard. Layer the Cheddar slices on top of the chutney sides, then the ham on top of that and pea shoots, if using. Cut into halves or quarters and serve.

How to sterilise jars:
Wash in hot, soapy water and rinse well. Stand on a baking sheet and place in an oven preheated to 140°C/120° fan/gas 1 for 15 minutes until completely dry. Fill and seal while still warm.

Mum's tip

Think about taking a little gift for your host. Flowers are great but require the host (who is already busy) to find something to put them in! So instead try something easy and personal: a small scented candle, pretty paper napkins, homemade marmalade, jam or pickles, or something sweet like biscuits always goes down well. If you do take flowers, then consider bringing them in a small jug or vase bought from a charity shop which can be as cheap as £1.

ROASTED PEPPER, MOZZARELLA & ROCKET

PREP: 10 minutes
COOKING: 25-30 minutes
MAKES 4

1 baguette
2 x 125g mozzarella balls
50g rocket
2 tsp balsamic glaze (see recipe above
 or use a good bought one!)

for the roasted peppers
3 red peppers
2 garlic cloves, crushed
2 tbsp olive oil
2 sprigs of rosemary, leaves chopped
salt and black pepper

Preheat the oven to 190°C/170°C fan/gas 5.

Cut the peppers into thick slices, about 3-4cm wide, and place all the peppers in a bowl.

Add the garlic, olive oil, rosemary and some salt and pepper and toss it all together, so that each pepper slice is coated in oil and herby seasoning. Tip out onto a baking tray or roasting tin and roast in the oven for 25-30 minutes, turning once or twice during cooking, until the pepper pieces are soft with blistered edges. Remove from the oven and leave to cool. You could also grill the peppers under a medium grill.

To assemble your sandwich, cut the baguette in half lengthways. Lay the slices of roasted pepper on the open bottom halves. Tear the mozzarella into chunks and lay over the peppers. Top with rocket and then drizzle over the balsamic glaze. Gently press the two halves of the sandwich together before using a serrated knife to cut the baguette into 4 large pieces.

HUMMUS, HALLOUMI, ROASTED RED PEPPER & BALSAMIC WRAP

PREP: 5 minutes (not including
 roasting the peppers)
COOKING: glaze 20-30 minutes,
 halloumi 6 minutes
MAKES 1

for the balsamic glaze
(or use a good bought one!)
3 tbsp soft brown sugar or honey
500ml balsamic vinegar

per wrap
$^1/_2$ tbsp olive oil
2 slices of halloumi
2 tbsp hummus
1 large seeded wrap
4 slices of roasted pepper (see below)
a small handful of baby spinach leaves

For the balsamic glaze, put the sugar or honey and vinegar in a small saucepan and stir to mix, then bring to the boil. Turn the heat down to low and allow to reduce for 20-30 minutes, until dark and sticky and reduced by half; it should coat the back of a metal spoon. Take it off the heat and allow it to cool completely before using. The glaze will keep in a jar in the fridge for several months.

For each wrap, heat the olive oil in a frying pan over medium-high heat, add your halloumi and fry for 2-3 minutes on each side, until slightly blistered and golden brown. Remove to a plate to cool slightly. Spread the hummus evenly over a wrap. Place the slices of roasted red pepper on top. Tear the cooked halloumi slices in half lengthways, then lay them in a line down the middle of your wrap. Top with the spinach and drizzle with the balsamic glaze. Tuck the bottom end of the wrap up then roll it up around the halloumi.

BAKED FILO CAMEMBERT WITH CRUDITÉS

This is really easy to make and you can't go wrong with melted cheese! It's best if you serve it on one platter and all dig in together round the table – scoop up the runny cheese with crunchy veg and fresh bread.

PREP: 15 minutes
COOKING: 20–25 minutes

SERVES 6

60g butter
1½ tbsp runny honey
4 sheets of filo pastry
1 whole Camembert (250g)

to serve
1 baguette,
    cut into slices
raw vegetable sticks

Preheat the oven to 200°C/180°C fan/gas 6 and remove any high shelves (to give your cheese enough headroom; it will be tall with the filo). Line a baking tray with non-stick baking paper.

Put the butter and honey in a small saucepan over a low heat and gently heat until just melted.

Lay one sheet of filo on a clean, dry work surface. Using a pastry brush, brush a thin, even layer of honey-butter mixture over the whole sheet, then lay a second sheet of filo on top, overlapping it at a 45° angle to the first. Lay the next one at a 45° angle to that one and repeat this process with the remaining sheet, so you have 4 overlapping layers of pastry fanning out.

Remove the packaging from the Camembert then, using a sharp knife, carefully cut a series of lines in the top of the cheese, in a criss-cross pattern and without going all the way through to the bottom. Place your cheese in the centre of your pastry. Using a gentle touch, gather the layers of pastry up over the top of the cheese, like wrapping a present. Gently press the pastry together to form a bunch over the top and straighten the pastry rising up from where you've gathered it. Brush the remaining melted honey-butter mixture all over the outside of the pastry, aiming to cover all the exposed bits.

Carefully lift the wrapped cheese and place on the lined baking tray. Bake for 15 minutes until the pastry is crisp and golden brown. If the pastry starts to brown too much, cover the top very loosely with a piece of tin foil for the remaining cooking time.

Serve with slices of baguette for mopping up and vegetable sticks for dipping in the melted cheese.

MY BIRTHDAY

I was always very lucky when I was growing up that my birthday and Easter would often fall days apart, which meant I could celebrate an entire day for my birthday during the holidays with my friends rather than just a couple of hours after school. One very memorable year we took a picnic basket down to the playing field on a surprisingly hot March day. It was full of all the essentials like party rings, sausage rolls, chocolate fingers, a bottle of prosecco and a litre of orange juice. We took loads of photos on disposable cameras, played games and had the best day. Not much changes really when it comes to my birthday now. I like to spend it with friends or family and keep it all quite relaxed. I don't tend to plan too much for my birthday, as I like to leave that down to my other half, who always seems to pull it out of the bag – I like to think he's picked up some tips from me over the years! One year he arranged a surprise afternoon tea at a nearby stately home and then everyone came back to ours for a takeaway and to watch movies all evening. We always make the morning of our birthdays special by laying out presents alongside breakfast, treats, a cake, balloons and decorations. I'll often have some close friends or family over too (maybe even staying over the night before) and it's such a nice way to start your birthday off! As long as I am surrounded by people I love, I will always have the best day.

As long as I am surrounded by people I love, I will have the best day.

Although I don't tend to do too much for my own birthday most years, birthdays are by far one of my favourite things to arrange and plan for other people! It's the one event that you can really tailor and personalise for a specific person, and this makes picking themes and decorations a lot easier and more fun. If you have a friend who loves festivals and their birthday falls in the summertime, you could attempt to create a mini festival in your back garden (see my garden party on pages 80–89 for ideas). Or if you have a friend who loves Halloween, decorate the house with spooky decorations, make a gruesome cake and plan a horror movie night! (See my Halloween section on pages 144–157 for some of my favourite spooky tips.) It's also fun to do something around the theme of music, using an era of music, a genre of music or asking people to come dressed as their favourite music artist. It also makes creating a playlist an extremely important aspect of the party!

When it comes to planning a birthday party, there are a few questions you need to ask yourself first:

HOW MANY PEOPLE AND WHEN?
Are you planning a big celebration or something more intimate? Consider how much time you have to plan the party, and get the invites out nice and early, especially if it's for a bigger party. If you don't have a lot of time to write invites, create an event on social media.

SURPRISE OR NOT?
This is a huge decision. If your birthday pal hates being the centre of attention, a surprise might lose you your bestie title! It's possible that once they've recovered from the initial embarrassment of being pounced on unawares they might warm up, but it's definitely worth considering whether this could be their worst nightmare, which would really spoil the mood. When inviting guests, you need to make it extremely clear if it is a surprise and if possible let them know as few details as you can, as it's all too easy to let these things slip. If you manage to pull off throwing a huge surprise party for someone you're very close to, you will automatically earn your hostess badge – but you will also feel a *huge* sense of relief and pride!

SPACE AND PLACE?

How much space will you need and where could you hold it? If you are planning a larger party with more than twenty guests, it's worth thinking about renting a space like a village hall, a room in a country house, a little café or part of a pub. If the weather is likely to be good, your local park, the beach or even your back garden are all great location options. Also think about what you want to do at the party – if you are planning on hiring a bucking bronco and a giant bouncy castle, or installing a piñata, then those things will definitely need more space!

ACTIVITY OR RELAXED SHINDIG?

What does the birthday girl or boy love most in the world? There are endless possibilities for things to do as birthday activities, and this is the fun part. For the slightly more laid-back, ideas such as flower arranging and floral crown making, pottery painting, spa days and beauty pamper sessions are all fun examples of what you and a group of friends could do. Alternatively, the more adventurous friend might like to go paintballing, do a watersports day, an escape room, life drawing, a ghost walk or an outdoor adventure activity swinging from trees, tied to ropes.

There is always the slightly easier option of making it a special night in. You could ask each attendee to bring their choice of alcoholic beverage while you supply the mixers and all have fun creating cocktails. Or grab throws and blankets, get in lots of popcorn and face masks and make a home cinema where you can all have a pamper sesh while watching your favourite 90s chick flick. Or I love any excuse for a pizza party! (See pages 130–133.)

DECORATION AND FOOD

One thing to remember when you are planning a birthday party is that most guests will be very happy to help you out if you need it. Where I find that many hands make light work is with two of the most important elements: food and decoration.

Decoration Number One that is a *must* whenever I am throwing a birthday shindig is BALLOONS – and lots of them. My favourites are the ones with written words and numbers and ones containing real foliage. I find it's nice to have a mix of lovely professional looking balloons – maybe some confetti-filled ones – alongside some slightly more basic ones that are just blown up by you and your friends, and scattered on chairs and the ground for a bit more decoration. It's also great to have some bunting hanging up or some paper garlands (see page 64 for my pretty paper chains). And don't forget to theme your decorations. Think about the person's favourite colours or maybe colours that might suit the theme a little better. Scary movie night? I'd use black, grey, red and orange as a base to decorate. When it comes to food, the smaller and more nibbly the better. Unless you have time among everything else to be whipping up a storm in the kitchen, it's all about finger food and things that are easy to cook and eat. Birthday snacks are some of my favourite – I still enjoy a party ring at twenty-eight and, nope, I'm not the only one!

THE CAKE

Every birthday needs a birthday cake, although it actually doesn't necessarily need to be a cake at all. One big centrepiece is always dreamy, especially if you've incorporated your colours and theme into it, but there are other ideas that might appeal more. You could go for a giant donut cake, a cupcake tower (great if you want to have multiple flavours or if some guests are dairy- or gluten-free), a pile of brownies covered in sprinkles or a huge stack of birthday pancakes with candles on top... get a bit creative with it and don't just feel you have to go with a giant Victoria sponge.

TIP

Decide where you want to spend or save. There may be certain things you think would really complement the party like professional balloons vs blowing up your own. Or maybe you'd prefer to spend more of your budget on a venue as opposed to using your own house!

Mum's tip

Grandad always made my birthday parties fun. He would build a coconut shy using planks of wood, cans and yoghurt pots, underneath the pots were sweets and we had to throw little bags of sand at the yoghurt pots to knock them down and get the sweets. You don't always need to buy everything, and sometimes even a cardboard box can become anything you want it to be (especially for younger children).

VEGGIE BREAKFAST

Lazy weekend breakfasts are a common occurrence in our house, and this veggie fry-up is often my go-to. Just put everything in bowls and let everyone help themselves. To make this suitable for vegans, leave out the halloumi and scramble tofu instead of eggs.

PREP: 20 minutes
COOKING: 30 minutes
SERVES 4

4 slices of sourdough bread
3 x 400g tins of baked beans
sea salt and black pepper
balsamic glaze, to drizzle (see page 52)

for the tomatoes
4 ripe tomatoes, halved crossways,
  or tomatoes on the vine
1 tbsp olive oil
2 sprigs of thyme, leaves only

for the spinach
260g spinach leaves
2 tbsp balsamic vinegar
1 tbsp sesame seeds, toasted
  (see page 43)
½ tbsp olive oil

for the zesty hummus
1 tub of hummus (about 300g)
juice of ½ lemon
½ tsp ground cumin

for the crushed avocado
2 ripe avocados
juice of ½ lime

for the halloumi
1 tbsp olive oil
1 x 250g block of halloumi, cut into 8 slices

for the scrambled eggs
10 large eggs
4 tbsp milk
a knob of butter

Get your tomatoes roasting and while they are cooking, prepare the rest of the breakfast. Preheat the oven to 180°C/160°C fan/gas 4. Lay the tomatoes cut side up on a baking tray. Drizzle with the olive oil, scatter over the thyme leaves and season with salt and pepper. Roast for 25 minutes, until the skins are wrinkled. Remove and keep warm.

Rinse the spinach in a colander under the cold tap. Heat a large frying pan over a medium-high heat. When the pan is hot, give the colander a few shakes, then tip the spinach into the pan. Add the balsamic vinegar and a pinch of salt. Allow the spinach to cook for 8-10 minutes until all the liquid has evaporated, stirring from time to time with a spoon. Add the toasted sesame seeds and olive oil, and stir to combine. Cook for another 1-2 minutes, then keep warm in the pan until serving.

Scoop the hummus into a little serving bowl and stir through the lemon juice and cumin. Taste it and if you think it needs a little more salt or pepper, go ahead and add it. Set the bowl to one side.

Cut the avocados in half and remove the stones. Scoop the flesh away from the skin with a spoon and place in a small bowl. Squeeze over the lime juice, add a pinch of salt and then mash together with a fork.

To cook your halloumi, heat the olive oil in a frying pan over a medium-high heat. Add the halloumi and cook for 2-3 minutes before turning over and cooking for another 2-3 minutes. The cheese should be golden and blistered, but not too melty. Remove from the heat and keep warm. (You can also grill it if you prefer.)

Break the eggs into a bowl and beat with a fork. Add the milk and season with salt and pepper then whisk with the fork to combine. Melt the butter in a frying pan over a medium-low heat. When the butter has melted, tip the eggs into the pan. Stir gently but constantly with a spoon to ensure an even consistency. Cook until the eggs are just set, with no visible uncooked white, but be careful not to over-scramble them.

Toast the bread and warm the beans just before serving everything in little bowls so your guests can help themselves. Drizzle with balsamic glaze (see page 52 to make your own – or buy a good one!).

SMOOTHIES

Smoothies are an easy way to contribute to your five a day – and they are so delicious.

Don't be put off by the chilli in the mango smoothie – it really works with the sweet mango and cooling yoghurt! The oaty smoothie is very filling – perfect for breakfast or as a snack if I have a busy day.

PREP: 5 minutes or less
EACH RECIPE MAKES
1 big smoothie, which is enough for 2.

MANGO, LIME & YOGHURT WITH A HINT OF CHILLI

2 ripe mangoes, peeled, stoned and cut into rough chunks (about 400g prepared weight)
juice of 4 limes
4 tbsp natural yoghurt
½ -1 fresh green Thai chilli, deseeded and roughly chopped

Instead of starting with whole mangoes, you can buy prepared mango pieces from the fresh snack section of the supermarket – perfect for smoothies!

Add the mango to the jug of your blender, then add the lime juice, yoghurt and as much chilli as you'd like. Blitz the whole lot together until smooth.

BERRY BLITZ WITH POMEGRANATE JUICE

200g mixed frozen berries (raspberries, blackberries and blackcurrants are perfect)
150ml pomegranate juice
½ banana
1 tbsp raspberry or strawberry jam

Add all the ingredients to the jug of your blender and whizz until smooth. The frozen berries make this quite a thick, refreshing smoothie. If you'd like it a little thinner, add another splash or two of pomegranate juice. Full of antioxidants and vitamin C, this will give you a real boost.

BANANA, MAPLE & OATS WITH CINNAMON

3 ripe bananas
50g rolled oats
3 tbsp maple syrup
½ tsp ground cinnamon
300ml milk of your choice

This is a great breakfast smoothie. Add all the ingredients to the jug of your blender and whizz until smooth.

CARROT, ORANGE & GINGER

2 medium carrots, peeled and coarsely grated
2 tsp grated fresh ginger
1 orange, peeled
1 banana
200ml apple juice

essential equipment:
a blender

Add the carrots to the jug of your blender, along with the ginger, orange and banana. Pour in the apple juice and whizz until smooth. Great for if you are feeling under the weather or if you need a pick me up.

BIRTHDAY PARTY PAPER CHAINS

Paper chains are the perfect party decoration. As they only involve some simple cutting and sticking, you can easily make a long length of paper chains while watching your favourite box-set!

You will need:

sheets of A4 coloured paper in three or four different shades
pencil
ruler
scissors
hot glue gun or double-sided sticky tape
washi tape or sticky tape

How to:

1 Using a ruler and pencil, draw a series of light pencil lines across the width of your sheets of A4 paper. I divided each sheet of A4 into 10 equal-sized strips (each strip was 2.9cm wide). Cut along these pencil lines to make strips of paper. Repeat until all the sheets of paper have been cut into strips.

2 Take one strip of paper and bend it into a ring. Using either a hot glue gun or double-sided sticky tape, fix the two short ends together.

3 Take another strip of paper, in another colour if you're using more than one shade, and loop the second strip through the paper ring you've just made with the first strip. Glue the short ends together to make another ring. Repeat with all the other strips until your paper chain is the right length.

4 On party day, decide where you want to hang your paper chains and fix each end to the wall with washi tape or sticky tape, adding in extra loops when necessary so the paper chain hangs in swags.

FOUR-TIER OMBRE BIRTHDAY CAKE

Ranging from light to dark, this cake covers lots of flavours – vanilla, caramel and both milk and dark chocolate. You can really go wild with the decorations and personalise it to suit who you are making it for by using their favourite chocolate bars on top! You can see the inside of the cake on page 71.

PREP: 45-60 minutes
COOKING: 40-50 minutes
COOLING: 1 hour

SERVES 10-12

for the top 2 cakes

250g unsalted butter, softened,
  plus extra for greasing
250g caster sugar
4 large eggs
2 tsp vanilla extract
250g self-raising flour
1 tsp baking powder
2 heaped tbsp caramel (from a tin)

for the bottom 2 cakes

100g milk chocolate, broken into chunks
150g dark chocolate, broken into chunks
250g unsalted butter, softened
150g golden caster sugar
100g dark muscovado sugar
4 large eggs
2 tsp vanilla extract
250g self-raising flour
1 tsp baking powder
3 tsp unsweetened cocoa powder

for the chocolate buttercream

400g milk chocolate, broken into chunks
400g unsalted butter
2 tsp vanilla extract
500g icing sugar
2 tbsp whole milk, if needed

essential equipment:

2 x 20cm round cake tins
stand mixer or electric beaters
piping bag fitted with a plain nozzle
cake leveller (for a pro finish!)
kitchen thermometer (if you are making the icing)

Preheat the oven to 180°C/160°C fan/gas 4. Grease and line 2 x 20cm round cake tins.

In the bowl of a stand mixer or in a mixing bowl using electric beaters, cream the butter and sugar for the top 2 cakes together until fluffy and light. Add your eggs, one at a time, beating well between each to incorporate fully. Add the vanilla extract. Combine the flour and baking powder together then, using a spoon, stir this through the batter. Spoon half the batter into one of the prepared tins and leave the other half in your mixing bowl. Add the caramel to the batter left in the mixing bowl and fold it well to mix it in. Spoon this caramel batter into the second prepared tin and level the tops of both mixtures in the tins with a spatula. Bake for 20-25 minutes, or until a toothpick inserted into the centre of each cake comes out clean. Leave the cakes to cool in their tins for a few minutes before turning out onto a wire rack to cool completely. When the tins are cool enough, wash, grease and line them again for your next cakes.

Melt the two types of chocolate in separate small heatproof bowls set over pans of simmering water, stirring occasionally until smooth and silky. Don't let the bottom of the bowls touch the hot water or you could burn the chocolate. Remove the bowls from the pans and allow to cool to room temperature.

Make your second batch for the bottom 2 cakes as you did for the first. Divide the mixture equally between two bowls. Stir the melted milk chocolate into one of the mixtures with 1 teaspoon of the cocoa powder, and spoon into one of your prepared tins. To the other bowl, add the melted dark chocolate and the remaining 2 teaspoons of cocoa powder, and fold well to combine. Spoon this darker batter into the second tin and smooth the mixture in both tins with a spatula. Bake for 20-25 minutes, turn out and cool as for the first batch.

For the buttercream, melt the milk chocolate as before. Remove the bowl from the pan and allow to cool to room temperature. (If you try to use the chocolate while it's too hot, you risk melting the butter.)

(recipe continued overleaf)

In the bowl of a stand mixer or in a mixing bowl using electric beaters, beat the butter and vanilla extract until soft and the butter has turned a creamy white colour – this can take anywhere from 5–10 minutes. Add the icing sugar one spoonful at a time, to avoid billowing clouds of icing sugar all over your kitchen. Once all the sugar has been incorporated, whip the mixture on a higher speed for a few minutes to add volume and lightness to the buttercream. Add the cooled melted chocolate, then whip again for several minutes to achieve a light, fluffy texture; it should be spreadable and soft, so if you think it's too stiff, add a little milk, a teaspoon at a time, to loosen it.

Choose a large plate or platter and place your darkest cake layer on, as the base. Add a generous blob of buttercream and spread it out with a flat knife or spatula. Add your milk chocolate cake layer, and another dollop of buttercream and spread out. Then add your caramel layer, repeating the buttercream, then top with your plain vanilla layer. Cover the cake in a thin, patchy layer of buttercream to act as a crumb coating. Chill the cake for 20 minutes to set the crumb coat, then cover the whole cake in another, thicker layer of buttercream, smoothing it all around with a flat knife or cake decorating tool. Add the remaining buttercream to a piping bag, fitted with a plain nozzle. Chill the cake for another 10 minutes to set the second layer, then you can go all out in personalising the decorations.

You can either use the buttercream in the piping bag like glue to cover the top of the cake with chocolate bars, wafers, chocolate curls and sweets – just pipe a little buttercream onto the backs of your chosen toppings and pile them high – or you can make an additional layer of shiny chocolate icing and stick the toppings to that (see below).

for the chocolate icing (optional)
160ml double cream
140g caster sugar
60g cocoa powder
3 gelatine leaves

to decorate
chocolate bars, chocolate curls,
sweets, biscuits, macaroons, etc.

To make the icing, gently heat all the ingredients along with 150ml water in a small saucepan. Stir until the sugar melts, then boil for 2 minutes. Remove from the heat and leave to cool for 15 minutes (if you have a kitchen thermometer, it should be no more than 38˚C). Meanwhile, soak the gelatine leaves in cold water for 5 minutes. Squeeze them to remove most of the water, then stir them into the cooled chocolate icing. Make sure the icing is really smooth. Pour your icing over the top of your cooled cake and let it drip down the sides! Then decorate with sweets and sparklers.

If you want your cakes to appear more neat and pro, before you assemble the cake and cover it with buttercream, finely slice off the harder outsides and the very top of the cake, making each layer uniform! You can use a wire cake leveller for this.

BIRTHDAY CAKE TOPPER

When it comes to birthday cakes, I don't think it's possible to be over-the-top! Instead of icing a message onto the cake, which is a really hard thing to get right, you can use a cake topper – it adds extra glitz and height and allows you to really personalise it for someone special (and if they are anywhere near as sentimental as I am they can then keep it).

You will need:

a piece of paper
pencil
a sheet of thick card
paper scissors and/or scalpel
glue stick and fine loose glitter
  (optional)
paper drinking straws
hot glue gun or sticky tape

How to:

1 First work out what message you want your topper to say. I've chosen 'Let's Party', because it works well with different occasions! Simple names and numbers work well too, or clearly readable shapes like hearts and balloons. Either write your message by hand or use a favourite font on your computer to print out the phrase. Experiment with the placement of the letters – if your message is two or more words, you might want to stack words on top of each other. And think about the way that the letters connect – each letter needs to link to the next so that you can cut it all from one piece of card.

2 Once you're happy with the placement of the letters (or shapes), you need to transfer it to the thick card for your topper. The easiest way to do this is to turn the piece of paper with your lettering on it over and gently scribble over the back with a soft pencil. Turn it back over (so it's the right way up), place it on top of your thick card and draw around your lettering with firm pressure. This will leave a rough outline of your lettering on your card. Carefully cut it out using scissors or a scalpel. You might find it easiest to cut away any sections in the centre of the message first before taking away the larger sections around the outside.

3 If you're using plain card, but want to add extra glittery shimmer, cover the cut card message with a thin layer of glue. Place the glue-covered card on some scrap paper and sprinkle over fine loose glitter. Leave to dry.

4 Take two paper straws and, using either a hot glue gun or strips of sticky tape, fix a straw to the back side of either end of the cut card message. Check from the front that the straws aren't too visible but look neat before sticking them in place.

5 Once your cake is baked and decorated, gently push the paper straws into the top layer of the cake, keeping the message nicely centred.

Sum

mer

It's finally summer: those long-awaited months that most of us absolutely pine for have arrived! For me, summer always represents parties and social gatherings. With long days, even longer summer evenings and with the weather (mostly) glorious, the possibilities for making plans are pretty much endless. Gone are those cosy, dark nights surrounded by all your most delicious smelling candles and lashings of comfort food. The layers are hung back up in the wardrobe and floaty florals and strappy sandals can finally make an appearance. I feel like most of my favourite memories are made in the summer months, as there is so much more to do and so many places to visit and explore. Everyone's moods are lifted by the injection of colourful food and sunshine on skin, and being able to lie out in the garden or in the park and really appreciate the outdoors.

One year, we went one step further and bought a waterslide and a giant paddling pool for the back garden – you can bet that even grown adults will have the BEST time playing at being big kids with water guns, water balloons and an inflatable pool to dip in and out of! Summer is also the season for barbecues, and this is one of my absolute favourite ways to dine – even if it is with a last-minute disposable barbecue and a mad dash around the supermarket to grab the last burger buns off the shelf!

Living near the sea has its huge perks in the summertime, with all the incredible ice-cream shops and the opportunity to eat fish and chips after work (provided you manage to avoid the greedy, guzzling seagulls, of course). Although the queues are longer and the beach is busier it's always worth it, as the atmosphere is that little bit more magical on summer evenings and you can end up losing track of time altogether. Local parks and pub gardens are buzzing too, with everyone keen to be outside as much as they can.

Summer is also the season for festivals and fruit picking, one of which, admittedly, I am much more comfortable with than the other! There really is nothing more therapeutic than strolling through fields of fresh fruit with your little basket and stocking up on more fruit than you could ever consume in one

> I feel like most of my favourite memories are made in the summer months.

season. I like using fresh fruit in flavoured waters too, for a refreshing summery drink – or you can also use it in a big jug of Pimm's (see pages 104–105).

I find that throwing parties and hosting guests in the summer is always so much easier. You don't have to think up ways to entertain guests indoors or how to defrost them after being out in the cold! You also have the freedom to host not only in your home but outside, giving the house a bit of a break and enabling the guest list to extend a bit. Similarly, gathering up friends to go for a picnic or to the beach means more space and fewer things to worry about, like spilling things on the carpet at home! For more relaxed and impromptu events like this, you can even ask everyone to bring something along, and everyone can help tidy up at the end as well! I do believe that summer is one of the best times of the year to don your hostess hat.

I love giving people the best experience and providing them with a good time, knowing they will go home happy.

If you're anything like me, though, you will thrive off hosting parties at home. I love giving people the best experience and providing them with a good time, knowing they will go home happy. We like to throw a big summery party every year and get everyone over – you can read more about it on pages 81–87. You can go a bit wilder with themed outdoor parties too, and lay on finger food and big salad bowls for everyone to help themselves. The decorations can be colourful and fun – and if all else fails, that paddling pool will be the best entertainment!

SUMMER TO-DO LIST

○ Create your summer playlist for garden parties, barbecues or road trips.

○ Whip out your body scrubs and body lotions – it's 'pins out' season!

○ Clean down your barbecue and have some frozen burgers and buns stashed away for the more-than-likely occasion you end up having a last-minute barbecue. Also, see my favourite picnic recipes on pages 114–123.

○ Dust off your picnic hamper and wash your picnic blankets.

○ Make plans with friends and family a little further in advance. Although summer is the most spontaneous season, it's also most people's busiest time, with holidays and weddings, so secure the dates while you can and send out any invites nice and early.

○ Stock up the freezer with ice creams and ice lollies. There comes a great satisfaction with being able to offer your guests their absolute favourite icy treat!

○ Make ice cream freakshakes (see page 134)!

○ Revamp the bar cart or alcohol stash! Summer beverages are so much fun to make with friends! Ensure you have Pimm's, lemonade and fruit at all times during the summer for those occasions your friends 'pop in', but end up staying all evening until the sun sets – see the drinks bar on pages 104–105 for more ideas.

○ Keep a list of all your favourite summer spots and, similarly, spots to avoid during peak season. I love visiting National Trust nature reserves and gardens in summer, as well as going on local walks and to pubs with good gardens.

○ Stock up on ice cubes. Lots of ice cubes.

○ Go on a bike ride.

○ Read a book in the garden.

○ Visit the beach as much as you can – see pages 110–111 for some beach picnic inspiration.

○ Play rounders with your friends.

Chill Tent

GARDEN PARTY

Garden parties are something that I'd longed to be able to host since I was a little girl, and as soon as I had my very own space of green, planning an outdoor party was one of the first things on my agenda!

We moved into our new home in the summer and I thought it would be a great idea to combine a house-warming with a summer garden party, thus making the house-warming 'garden' themed. (It also meant guests were mostly outside, which eliminated fear of footprints or spilt drinks on new rugs and carpets!) Living in the UK, you do have to settle for the fact that the big day could arrive hand in hand with a rain cloud. I checked the weather an obsessive amount leading up to our party, but no amount of checking will ever give you a proper answer, so you just have to commit but be open to changing plans slightly and dashing inside at the last minute, or having a back-up plan in case the skies open! We ended up hiring a stretch tent just in case, and it was the best decision we made as it actually rained A LOT! We set up the tent a day or so before and made it super-cosy inside with blankets and cushions and masses of fairy lights. We strung up as many as we could – it took five of us a good couple of hours the night before; it was so magical seeing them all lit up as it started to get dark. We also spent hours unfolding paper decorations in varying shades of green and white and hung them from the tent too. (These ended up being rained on and hung all saggy and dripping green dye, but the thought was there!)

It goes without saying that if you want to throw a party, then the first thing you need to do is set a date and make a list of the people you want to invite. Consider whether it is going to be a plus-one party, or more of a close friend kind of gathering. The size of your garden and the amount of food and drink you feel able to supply are likely to be key in making these decisions. I like to let people know what kind of party it is going to be on the invitation, so the next thing to consider is the theme. Then you can design or choose your invitations to match. Since ours was 'garden' (which is a pretty straightforward concept considering that was exactly what it was!) we designed our invites online and added a few green touches. Use your imagination and choose whatever theme you think you and your guests will enjoy. For my friend Poppy's birthday last year, we set up a tropical theme with lots of palm trees, flamingos and pineapples – it was also a very easy theme to grab decorations and set a menu for. It's also a great one to do in summer as the costumes can be so vibrant and colourful.

> As soon as I had my very own space of green, planning an outdoor party was one of the first things on my agenda!

Remember that people get booked up really quickly during the summer months, so get formal invites out as early as you can, by post, email, social media or text, and always state a date for the RSVP so you know how many people are going to come. It's good to give people a friendly reminder around a week before, so you can double check whether your guests can still attend or if something else has cropped up.

One of my favourite things we did at our party was to use chalkboards as signs (see page 97), dotted around the garden pointing people in the direction of the toilet, the trampoline and the table tennis table for a spot of ping pong or beer pong!

Even though it rained... A LOT... it was one of the best parties we had ever thrown and everyone had a great time. I can't wait for next year!

WHAT TO CONSIDER WHEN THROWING A GARDEN PARTY

THE NUMBER OF GUESTS, THE INVITES AND YOUR BUDGET

If you are having more than fifty guests it might be a good idea to call in some extra help, especially with the food. You can maybe even ask a few guests who don't mind a spot of cooking to bring along their signature dishes. My mum makes a great coronation chicken, so she was more than willing to cook and bring some with her! Maybe think about hiring someone to work the bar if your budget allows. Another way to manage a larger gathering – if it's starting to feel a bit overwhelming – is to ask if a few of your close friends might like to get involved too. Splitting up a few tasks can really help ease the stress, and it's fun to plan together! It is also courteous to give your neighbours a heads-up that you will be having people over and playing music. Keep everyone in the loop so people can be prepared. If your party is big enough maybe even extend the offer for them to pop over for a drink!

WEATHER

You need a plan B should it decide to rain. Could you get everyone inside? If that's not an option, have a look at hiring something like a stretch tent, a gazebo or a bell tent, or even making your own cover! Be careful if you are going to hire a gazebo though, as a surprising number aren't waterproof (I found this out the hard way).

FOOD AND DRINK

When it comes to food and drink, I think it's best to keep it quite relaxed so you don't get too stressed in the lead up. I also see nothing wrong with cutting a few corners here and there and buying in some extras! Big bowls of fresh, colourful salads or a barbecue with plates of side dishes is the easiest way to feed lots of people. Be sure to plan for plenty of options to cater for people's different needs – think about including vegan and vegetarian options, and some sweet treats.

If you're going to do a barbecue, it might be worth asking someone to be in charge of it. And they should be aware that that will be their station for the food portion of the evening! You should think slightly ahead when it comes to the food – a lot of finger food and salads can be prepared in advance, for instance. Don't leave it until the morning of the party before popping along to your local supermarket in the hope they will have twenty hotdog buns in the middle of summer. If you are strapped for time, you can do a food shop online. It also makes life a lot easier to have things delivered directly to you, including an order of ice on the day.

When I think of a garden party I immediately think of a jug of Pimm's or a beautifully decorated cocktail. Set up a drinks table somewhere out of the sun, so people can help themselves – just keep an eye on it to make sure it is kept well stocked. (See my recipes on pages 104–105.) We saved most of our ice for the cocktails, but we also filled a wheelbarrow with it and put lots of glass bottles of cola, lemonade and beers in it for guests to help themselves to throughout the day. Be sure to remember to attach a bottle opener to the wheelbarrow – we forgot this, so it meant people kept having to ask, which sort of defeated the whole purpose of it being help yourself! We also filled three giant water dispensers with flavoured water and stacked outdoor glasses next to it. If there's a lot of alcohol flowing, you need to make sure there is something to hydrate everyone.

SERVING THE FOOD

For a smaller number of people, you can use your regular plates, knives and forks, but if you have a larger group of guests coming, you need to make a plan as eating potato salad with your hands off a paper napkin can be really messy! One thing you can do is rally round your friends and family and borrow as much as you can. You can also hire it, or buy picnic-

Mum's tip

Once you have set a date
for an event and invited your
guests, the fun begins. Many
times I've sat in the bath (peace
and quiet!) surrounded by Delia,
Nigel, Nigella and Jamie poring
through their books and
working out the perfect
menu.

style plates and serving dishes – or even pretty paper plates! We decided to buy picnic plates and cutlery as we knew we would re-use them for other garden parties.

DECORATION AND ATTENTION TO DETAIL

The decoration is an important aspect of any shindig, but when it's in the garden you have a bit more to play with as you have trees and hedges and elements of the outdoors that you can use to your advantage. My friend Poppy and I decorated a chalk sandwich board with a big 'Welcome to our garden party' message which sat by the gate so that as people arrived they were greeted without me having to stand there and direct them in. On the other side of the sign, which people saw as they left, we put taxi numbers and a little 'Thanks for coming'. I also strung fairy lights in as many places as I possibly could. The big festoon lights look amazing on something like a tent or the entrance to a conservatory or gazebo, but little copper wire battery lights are great to twist into small bushes and hedges just to add a bit of sparkle. If you are using anything that requires electricity, do make sure you have proper extension leads and make sure they are covered up so people don't trip over them – and of course don't let anything electrical get wet if it rains!

Inside the tent, we used very cheap and second-hand rugs and throws to line the ground and scattered giant cushions around the tables so that everyone was comfortable. We hung paper decorations anywhere we could, from the tent and in the trees. And we strung up bunting everywhere (see page 90 for how to make your own tropical garland). You can even add elements of detail to your food – we had little plant-style labels on little garden-themed cupcakes in plant pots so everyone knew what the flavours were. We also put disposable cameras on the tables so people could take their own photos of the party, and getting

(see page 90 for how to make your own tropical garland)

those developed weeks later was a great reminder of how much fun we had. Tiny jars of flowers always look so pretty displayed on tables. Tea lights, outdoor candles and lanterns are also must-haves; when the evening starts to draw in, it makes everything so cosy. Even in the height of summer, there will always be a bit of a chill in the air, and if you're planning on having quite a late one but staying in the garden, consider piling up a few throws for people to wrap around themselves, or even getting a fire pit to toast marshmallows over!

MUSIC AND FUN

It's important that with any party you create a bit of atmosphere with some great music and things to do. Create a playlist of some of your favourite summer tunes or ask guests to give you their favourite song when you send out the invites, so you can create a playlist of everyone's recommendations. There are so many outdoor games you can play, like giant Jenga, rounders or hoopla. My boyfriend has a ping-pong table, so this provided hours of entertainment with beer pong!

CLEARING OUT AND CLEARING UP

It's a good idea to set an end time for your garden party, so you don't have any stragglers while you're trying to keep your eyes open. Decide how much or how little you want to clear away that night – and how much you're willing to leave until the next day. Things like wrapping up leftover food and popping it in the fridge can't be left until the morning, but there's no point taking down all the fairy lights at 1am. I always think it's nice to have a couple of your nearest and dearest staying over the night of the party, so that you can have helpers the next morning, and can all make breakfast together and reminisce on the events of previous night before all parting ways.

Mum's tip

Ensure you have plenty of toilet roll and keep spares close by! It's also worth thinking about having a few fresh hand towels for the bathroom, as a damp one won't be of good use to anyone.

TROPICAL LEAF GARLAND

EXTRA EFFORT

This pretty garland is made from felt and doesn't even require any sewing skills. Drape it around the edge of your tables or hang it up like bunting.

You will need:

a few sheets of paper
pencil
paper scissors
sheets of coloured felt in shades of
   green, yellow, pink and any other
   tropical colours of your choice
dressmaker's chalk pencil
fabric scissors
polyester or cotton twine in the colour
   of your choice
small push pins or drawing pins
   (optional)

How to:

1 Draw a template on paper for each leaf shape that you plan to cut for your garland. You can search for 'tropical leaf template' online and download a free template if you aren't confident in your drawing skills. I cut two different leaf shapes in two different sizes (my large leaves are 35cm tall by 25cm wide, while my smaller leaves are 23cm tall by 17cm wide). Once you're happy with the size and shape of your leaves drawn or printed onto paper, cut around the outline with paper scissors.

2 Take a sheet of felt in a colour of your choice and, using dressmaker's chalk pencil (which can be brushed away later), trace around your paper template, including any areas inside the leaf shape that you want to cut away.

3 Using fabric scissors, carefully cut around the chalk outline and snip away any extra decorative holes inside the leaf shape. Repeat with the other sheets of felt to make as many leaves as you plan for your garland. I cut out 12 large and 20 smaller leaves.

4 Once all the leaves have been cut from felt, lay them out to decide the order you want them in for the garland. I interspersed two smaller leaves between each large leaf – I also added in the odd white and yellow frangipani flower here and there for extra interest.

5 Next, you need to string your leaves onto the twine. Place a leaf flat in front of you. Now snip two small, vertical and parallel slits 1cm apart in the top-left part of the leaf. Do the same in the top-right part of the leaf, so you have a set of small slits on either side of the stem. Make sure they are level with each other so that the leaf will hang straight. Thread the twine through these slits; the side of felt where most of the twine is showing will be the back. Once all the felt leaves are threaded onto the twine, arrange the leaves as you want them – I prefer them slightly overlapping for a lusher jungle feel!

6 Decide where you want to hang your garland and tie the end of the twine securely to hold the weight of the felt leaves. Use small push pins or drawing pins, if you want to add some extra holding points along your garland.

CHICKEN QUINOA SALAD WITH FRESH HERBS

When it comes to feeding a crowd, salads are a quick win as everyone can help themselves. This is a really great fresh recipe and a crowd-pleaser in my house and a great way to use up leftover cooked chicken (or you can buy pre-cooked chicken to save time). It is also just as delicious without the chicken if you want to make a vegan version.

PREP: 35 minutes
COOKING: 2 hours
(if roasting the chicken)

SERVES 6–8 as a side dish

1 lemon, halved
1 chicken (1.5–2kg)
5 sprigs of thyme
4 tbsp olive oil
2 onions, thinly sliced
2 medium courgettes, thinly sliced
120g quinoa
360ml water
25g parsley, leaves roughly chopped
10g coriander, leaves roughly chopped
10g dill, leaves roughly chopped
40g pistachio kernels, roughly
  chopped
100g flaked almonds, toasted
100g pomegranate seeds
130g mixed rocket and watercress
sea salt and black pepper

for the dressing
2 tbsp pomegranate molasses
2 tbsp red wine vinegar
2 tsp English mustard
4 tbsp olive oil

Preheat the oven to 180°C/160°C fan/gas 4.

Squeeze the lemon juice over your whole chicken then put the squeezed halves and 2 of the thyme sprigs into the bird's cavity. Brush the outside of the chicken with 2 tablespoons of the oil and season it generously all over with salt and pepper. Strip the thyme leaves from the remaining sprigs and sprinkle them over the chicken, then place in a roasting tin and pop in the oven to roast for 30 minutes per 500g – so a 1.5kg chicken will take 1½ hours. To test the chicken is done, cut into the crease where the leg joins the breast – if the juices run clear, it's perfect.

Remove the tin from the oven and allow the chicken to rest for a few minutes before shredding it with two forks and piling the meat on a plate or platter. You need 500g.

Heat your remaining 2 tablespoons of olive oil in a large frying pan over a medium heat and fry the onion for about 8 minutes, or until it begins to soften. Add the courgette, season generously with salt and pepper and fry for 20–30 minutes. Both the onion and the courgette should be very soft, any liquid should have evaporated and the onion should be nice and brown. Remove from the heat and allow to cool to room temperature.

Tip your quinoa into a medium saucepan, cover with the water, bring to the boil then reduce the heat to low and cook for 15–20 minutes, until all the water has been absorbed. Remove from the heat and allow the quinoa to cool slightly.

Make the dressing by whisking all the ingredients together in a small bowl, seasoning with salt and pepper. Pour this into a little serving jug.

Assemble the salad by gently tossing the onions and courgette in a large bowl with the quinoa, chopped herbs, pistachios and almonds. Add the chicken and toss through the pomegranate seeds, rocket and watercress just before serving. Dress the salad with a spoonful or two of the pomegranate dressing – add more if you like, but it's wise to start with just a little.

FABRIC TASSEL GARLAND

If you're feeling crafty in the run-up to your celebration, this fabric tassel garland is a fun way to add a bit of colour to your party setting! It's also a great way to bring a theme to life.

You will need:

55 x 25cm (per tassel) lightweight polyester or cotton fabric
ruler
pencil
fabric scissors
polyester or cotton twine
hot glue gun (optional)
small push pins or drawing pins (optional)

How to:

1 Decide on the length of garland you want to make to work out how many tassels you will need. These tassels (pictured opposite) are 27.5cm long and are spaced 10cm apart, so for each metre of garland, there are 10 tassels.

2 Take one piece of fabric and fold it in half lengthways. Measure 4cm down from the folded edge and draw a line all the way across, parallel to the fold.

3 Using fabric scissors if you have them, cut the fabric from the unfolded edge up to the line to make lots of narrow flowing strips of fabric that are still attached at the top. These cuts are spaced 1.5cm apart. Make sure that you cut through both layers of fabric.

4 Open out the folded fabric so that the cut strips are now either side of the uncut centre. Starting at one end, roll the fabric up tightly along the length. The cut strips will tangle up a little, but don't worry, just try to make the uncut centre nice and tightly rolled.

5 Shake out the cut strips to untangle any that have become knotted, then fold the rolled-up fabric in half, along the uncut centre, so that all the strips are together again. Pull out one strip from the bundle and wrap it tightly around the top of the tassel leaving a small gap just above where the cuts start so that you can thread your twine through the loop when you hang them up; tie to secure.

6 Repeat the above steps with each piece of fabric until you have enough tassels for your garland, then thread the tassels onto the twine, passing the twine through the loop at the top of each tassel. To keep each tassel in place on the twine, you can add a small dab of glue from a hot glue gun to secure; you may not need to do this if your tassels sit snugly on your twine.

7 Decide where you want to hang your garland and tie the end of the twine securely to hold the weight of the fabric tassels. Use small push pins or drawing pins if you want to add some extra holding points along your garland.

CHALKBOARD SIGNS

At my summer party, we made a few chalkboard signs to direct people to various key areas of the garden. As well as being really nice extra decorations they are also very useful as people won't be asking you where the toilets are all the time, so leaving you free to enjoy the party!

You will need:

chalkboards in different sizes
chalks or a chalk pens
twine or ribbon to hang your signs if
    they don't come with stands

How to:

1 First decide what you want your signs to say. Good suggestions include: 'welcome to the garden party' (we then wrote 'thanks for coming!' on the other side so people would see it on their way out), 'this way to the bar', 'drinks this way', 'garden games' or 'to the toilet'.

2 Using your chalk or chalk pen, lightly sketch out on your chalkboard where you want your lettering to go. Think about using different fonts and different-sized letters for contrast, and also where you could add some embellishments such as leaves or birds. Leave space for an arrow if you need to direct people somewhere! Have a look online for some inspiration before you get going.

TIP

- Shadows on your letters look really effective.
- For larger designs, print out a template.
- To trace your template, cover the reverse with chalk, then turn it over and place it on your chalkboard and draw around the letters with a pen or pencil applying firm pressure. The chalk on the back will leave rough outlines on your chalkboard.
- Use different coloured chalk pens.

ZESTY TIGER PRAWN SKEWERS WITH LIME AIOLI

Prawns are a huge hit with so many of my friends and family in summertime. This aioli also makes a great dip for potato wedges.

PREP: 20 minutes
COOKING: 6–8 minutes

SERVES 8–10

400g (shelled but tail still
   intact) tiger prawns,
   defrosted overnight
   in the fridge if frozen
2 limes, cut
   into wedges
1–2 tsp vegetable oil
salt and black pepper

for the lime aioli
150g mayonnaise
1–2 garlic cloves
finely grated zest
   and juice of 2 limes
1 tsp Dijon mustard
salt and black pepper

for the marinade
3 garlic cloves,
   finely grated
finely grated zest
   and juice of 2 limes
salt and black pepper

essential equipment:
skewers

If you're using wooden skewers, soak them for 30 minutes before you use them, to ensure they don't burn.

Begin by making the aioli. Put the mayo into a small mixing bowl and finely grate in one of the garlic cloves. Add the lime zest and juice and the mustard and whisk the mixture together to combine. Taste – it should be garlicky and zesty, so if you think it needs another garlic clove or squeeze of lime, go for it. Season with salt and pepper and spoon into a pretty serving bowl.

For the marinade, put the garlic, lime zest and juice into a shallow bowl and season well with salt and pepper. Add your prawns, toss to coat them in the marinade and allow them to sit for 10 minutes.

Heat a griddle pan or the barbecue until very hot. Thread the prawns onto wooden skewers – if you are making them for a crowd as part of a party buffet, snap long skewers in half and thread 2 prawns onto each half skewer. Poke a wedge of lime onto each skewer.

Dab the vegetable oil onto a wad of kitchen paper and wipe over the griddle pan or barbecue grate, just to give it a light coating. Grill the skewers for 2–3 minutes per side, or until the prawns are bright pink and have firmed up.

Serve on a big platter with the aioli for dipping. The hot lime wedges on each skewer are great for squeezing over the top, too.

SHREDDED RED CABBAGE SALAD

This is a sweet crunchy salad. It's great for a garden party, but it's actually really nice with burgers and sausages at a regular barbecue too.

PREP: 20 minutes

SERVES 6-8
as a side dish

½ red cabbage
2 medium carrots
2 spring onions, trimmed
6 pitted Medjool dates
2 tbsp sesame seeds, toasted (see page 43)
2 tsp Dijon mustard (or another hot mustard to make it vegan)
2 tbsp cider vinegar
1 tsp caster sugar
75ml olive oil
1 dessert apple
salt and black pepper

Begin by removing the core of your cabbage and finely shredding the rest. Add it to a large mixing bowl. Peel and coarsely grate the carrots and finely slice the spring onions. Add them both to the bowl too. Cut the dates in half lengthways, then slice them into chunky matchsticks. Toss them and the toasted sesame seeds with the other vegetables in the bowl.

In a small bowl, whisk together the mustard, vinegar and sugar. Pour in the olive oil in a steady stream, whisking all the time. Season well with salt and pepper.

Dress the salad with the vinaigrette, season with salt and pepper, toss well to combine and allow it to rest for a few minutes. Just before serving, coarsely grate your apple directly into the bowl and then toss it through the dressed salad. Serve at room temperature.

SMOKY POTATO SALAD

Knowing how to make a potato salad is great to have under your belt. This one uses a slightly smoky, spicy chipotle paste – but you can leave that out if you prefer.

PREP: 10 minutes
COOKING:
20–25 minutes
COOLING:
20 minutes

SERVES 6–8
as a side dish

4 rashers of smoked streaky
  bacon (optional)
500g small new potatoes
1 small red onion, thinly
  sliced
1 red Romano pepper (or a
  regular pepper, if you can't
  find Romano), thinly sliced
25g chives, finely chopped
2 tbsp good quality
  mayonnaise
1 tbsp crème fraîche
1–2 tsp chipotle paste
juice of ½ lime
salt and black pepper

If you're including the bacon, begin by frying the rashers in a frying pan over a medium-high heat for 10–12 minutes until nice and crispy, turning them during cooking. Remove from the pan and allow to cool.

Wash the potatoes in cold water and cut any larger ones in half or thirds. You're aiming for them to all be roughly the same size. Add the potatoes to a large pan and cover them in cold water. Add a generous pinch of salt and bring to the boil. Cook the potatoes for 10–15 minutes, depending on size, or until you can pierce them easily with a fork. Drain into a colander and rinse briefly under the cold tap. Allow the potatoes to cool and drain well for at least 20 minutes, ideally to room temperature.

Put the sliced onion and pepper into a mixing bowl and add the chives. Tip in the cooled potatoes, then add the mayo, crème fraîche, 1 teaspoon of the chipotle paste and the lime juice. Season the whole lot well with salt and pepper, then toss all the ingredients together to coat. Taste it and if you'd like it a little spicier, add a little more chipotle paste.

Tip into a serving bowl and, if you're including the bacon, crumble it up with your fingers over the top of the salad before serving. If you're serving this to a mixed crowd of vegetarians and meat eaters, you could always serve the crumbled bacon in a separate bowl for people to add to their own servings.

THE DRINKS BAR

Drinks are an obvious essential for any party or event! I've listed some of my go-tos that people always love (and some non-alcoholic options for the drivers and non-drinkers).

GIN COCKTAIL

SERVES 1

50ml gin
ice cubes
150ml elderflower tonic water
1 slice of pink grapefruit
a sprig of rosemary
a sprig of mint
a few juniper berries (optional)

Pour the gin into a pretty glass, with a cube or two of ice, and add the elderflower tonic water. Squeeze the grapefruit slice slightly before adding it and the herb sprigs to the glass.

Serve with a few juniper berries in the glass, to bring out the aromatics of the gin, if you like.

TIP

Before adding the mint sprigs, be sure to give the mint leaves a little whack to extract the oil and provide maximum flavour.

PITCHER OF PIMM's

SERVES 3–4

½ cucumber
ice cubes
6 large strawberries, sliced
1 orange, sliced
3 sprigs of basil
3 sprigs of mint
250ml Pimm's No. 1
700ml sparkling lemonade

Use a vegetable peeler to peel the cucumber into long ribbons. Put some ice cubes in a large pitcher, then top with your sliced fruit and cucumber. Add the herbs, then pour in the Pimm's, followed by the lemonade. Give it a little stir with a long spoon and serve cold.

To make this non-alcoholic, replace the Pimm's with 100ml cold English breakfast tea, 50ml cranberry juice and 100ml ginger beer. Pour over the ice, fruit and herbs, followed by 700ml lemonade, as above. It's just as delicious!

Mum's tip

Always give your guests a drink when they arrive!

TROPICAL SLUSHIE

SERVES 1

120g pineapple (the ready-chopped chunks from the cold snack section of the supermarket are perfect)
juice of 1 lime
50ml coconut water
25ml white rum (optional)
a mugful of ice cubes
a sprig of mint

Add the pineapple, lime juice, coconut water, white rum (if using) and ice to a power blender and blitz on a high speed until you achieve the consistency of a slushie. If you think it needs more ice, then feel free to whizz some more in. Pour into a glass and serve straight away, with a sprig of mint. Leave out the rum for a refreshing soft drink!

MOJITO

SERVES 3-4

3-4 sprigs of mint
3 tsp demerara sugar
25ml lime juice (from 1-2 limes), plus a lime wedge
3-5 ice cubes
50ml white rum
150ml club soda

Pick the leaves from 3 of the mint sprigs and add them to your glass with the sugar and lime juice. Muddle them with a cocktail muddle, or bash them about with a small wooden spoon. You're looking to crush the mint, sugar and lime together to release all their oils and flavours. Add the ice and lime wedge and pour over the rum. Top the drink up with club soda. Serve with an additional sprig of mint, if you like.

TIP
Try making this with ginger beer instead of club soda, and leave out the rum for a virgin mojito.

FRUIT-INFUSED WATER

SERVES 3-4

Fruit, berries, spice and vegetable suggestions:
citrus (limes, oranges, lemons, grapefruit, bergamot), blueberries, strawberries, raspberries, grapes, fresh ginger, cucumber, kiwi, melon (cantaloupe, watermelon, honeydew), apple, pear, chilli, pineapple, pomegranate seeds

Herb suggestions:
mint, rosemary, basil, thyme, lemon thyme, lemon verbena, tarragon, lemongrass

ice cubes

Wash and slice whole fruit and berries, then add a selection, with whole herbs, to a large pitcher, or a large glass if you're making it for one person. Top up with cold or room temperature water and allow to infuse for about 30 minutes before adding ice and serving. You can keep the infusion in the fridge for up to 24 hours.

Strawberries, basil, mint and cucumber are a nice combo. So too are rosemary, lemon and apple.

SUMMER HERB GARDEN

Making your own indoor windowsill herb garden means your kitchen will smell amazing and you will always have fresh herbs to hand. You can use fresh herbs in salads (see pages 42, 93 and 118) or even in cocktails and flavoured waters (see pages 104-105) for impromptu gatherings. If you want to be really thrifty then you could even use large empty pasta sauce jars – just soak off the labels and wash them thoroughly before planting up. These would also make lovely gifts.

You will need:

glass jars with a wide neck (ideally at least 20cm deep to allow for the roots to grow)
a few pebbles or some gravel or marbles to provide drainage
potting compost
potting grit
plug-plants of your chosen herb (available from garden centres and mail-order suppliers)
plant labels
pen
string or twine
scissors

Good herbs to grow:

• Basil
• Chives
• Coriander
• Dill
• Lemon thyme
• Marjoram
• Mint
• Oregano
• Parsley
• Rosemary
• Tarragon
• Thyme

How to:

1 Fill the bottom of your jar with the pebbles, gravel or a few marbles.

2 Mix a small handful of potting grit into the compost. (For plants that prefer their roots to be kept quite dry, this helps to keep the soil free-draining.) Part-fill the jar with this compost mixture, leaving enough room for the plug-plant.

3 Carefully remove any packaging from the plant. Lift it into the soil-filled jar and position it centrally in the neck of the jar. If you need to, dig a little hole in the centre of the soil to make sure the plant's roots aren't too squashed in.

4 Fill the gaps around the plug-plant in the jar with the remaining potting compost. Aim to have the roots of the plug-plant beneath the soil and the green shoots above the level of the compost. You need to leave some space at the top of the jar for watering, so don't fill it with soil right to the very top. Once the soil has been added, press it down firmly all around the base of the plant to secure.

5 Immediately water the jar to give the herb plant a good drink.

6 For an added touch, tie plant labels around the jars and write the name of the herb on each one!

7 Place the jar in a sunny spot near a window where they'll get lots of natural light. Keep the jar watered, but be careful not to overwater – the soil should be moist but never soggy. Too little water and the herbs will wilt, but too much water and their roots will rot, so find the right balance.

8 A weekly feed of indoor plant food and an occasional shower from the tap or hose in the sink will keep your herbs happy. However, if a plant does begin to look straggly, then lift the roots out of the soil and re-pot the plant using fresh potting compost. Or if the herb plants outgrow the jars, replace them with fresh plug-plants and transplant the original herb plants into larger pots outdoors.

BEACH BBQ

Whether you live beside the sea or not, there will be those days of the year when it's so hot - and you know there's going to be an amazing sunset in the evening - that you pack up your towel and head to the nearest seaside spot with a couple of your friends.

On those days, you want to be sure you're making the absolute most of it and don't arrive having forgotten something vital. Living near the coast, these evenings are some of my absolute favourites and although most of the time they are completely spontaneous, there are definitely things you can do and bring to make it that little bit more special.

Traditionally, when I think of a picnic, I think of luscious green fields and daisy meadows with checked blankets and wicker baskets, but there is no reason why this can't shift to a seaside setting. If anything, I think it's slightly more magical as you have the sounds of the sea and the hustle and bustle of the beach. You do have to be a little wary of seagulls though!

If you decide that you want to do a barbecue beach picnic, you need to make sure the area of the beach you are sitting on will allow you to do this and that you don't pick a spot where pets and barbecues are banned; it's also polite to avoid lighting a barbecue directly upwind of other people. Mini burgers and kebabs are a must (see my recipes on the coming pages). Or, if you're buying it in, then go for food that is easy to eat with your hands, as you don't want anything too messy or that will require loads of plates and cutlery and washing up afterwards.

You could even make everyone their own 'lunchbox' so you don't have to serve food onto separate plates down at the beach - it's like a ready meal but wholesome, healthy and a lot more fun. Make sure that any meat you are planning to cook later in the day is transported in cool bags with plenty of freezer blocks to keep it chilled.

You should also be aware that anything you take to the beach must be taken home with you as you don't want to add to the overflowing bins, or create excessive waste and plastics that could end up in the sea. If everyone was a little more mindful of that, it could make a lot of difference during those peak months when the beaches are a lot more busy.

One thing you should definitely bring with you are a couple of good throws or blankets, not just to sit on, but to wrap up in as the sun goes down. And I also tend to take a bluetooth speaker to play music on - but always be considerate of those around you and only play it if people aren't close by. I like walking along the beach during summer and passing groups of people playing their music - it's like a very varied playlist that follows you as you go! If there is a larger group of people, maybe take some games along or something up your sleeve in terms of entertainment.

> You have the sounds of the sea and the hustle and bustle of the beach.

PICNIC LIST

- Picnic basket.
- Portable barbecue.
- Lighter or matches for barbecue.
- Cool bags and freezer blocks to keep drinks and food (especially if it's uncooked) chilled.
- Blankets to sit on and throws to cover up with in the evening.
- Cutlery - not disposable!
- Food in 'lunchboxes' or bento boxes.
- A bin liner for any rubbish to take home.
- Bluetooth speaker and your summer playlist.
- Camera.
- Games.
- A favourite ice-cream spot or sit near an ice cream van for a post dinner treat!

MINI CHEESEBURGERS WITH RED ONION RELISH

These adorable little burgers are ideal for a beach picnic and are great alongside the halloumi skewers on page 121. If you can't find mini burger buns they also work really well inside pitta breads with salad. I love this sticky, sweet onion relish on just about everything... try it with barbecued sausages too!

PREP: relish 5 minutes,
burgers 25 minutes
COOKING:
relish 25 minutes
burgers 10–15 minutes

MAKES 12

for the onion relish
25g butter
1 tbsp olive oil
2 red onions, thinly sliced
3 sprigs of thyme, leaves chopped
1 tbsp light muscovado sugar
2 tbsp red wine vinegar
salt and black pepper

for the burgers
1 tbsp olive oil
1 onion, finely chopped
800g lean minced beef
2 garlic cloves, minced
1 egg
1 tsp Worcestershire sauce
1 tsp light soy sauce
a little vegetable oil

to serve
100g sliced Monterey Jack cheese, each cut into 4
12 mini burger buns or pittas
12 slices of burger cheese
iceberg lettuce, shredded
ketchup and/or mustard

For the onion relish:
Begin by making your onion relish. Add the butter and olive oil to a frying pan over a medium heat and, when the butter has melted, add the sliced onions and thyme. Season with salt and pepper and cook for 15–20 minutes, stirring frequently, until the onions are soft and coloured. Add the sugar and vinegar and stir to dissolve the sugar. Allow to cook and reduce for a few minutes more, then take off the heat. You can use the relish once it's cool, or put in a jar in the fridge for later.

For the burgers
Heat the olive oil in a frying pan over a medium heat. Add the chopped onion with a pinch of salt and cook for 10–15 minutes or until the onion is meltingly soft and golden. Remove from the heat to cool slightly.

Put the beef mince, garlic, egg, Worcestershire and soy sauces into a large mixing bowl, tip the cooled onions into the bowl as well, and mix the ingredients together with your hands. Form the meat into 12 equal-sized patties and flatten them slightly in your palm. You can now chill them on a plate covered in a layer of baking paper in the fridge, until you're ready to cook either at home or on the beach.

Preheat a barbecue or griddle pan to a high heat. Brush the grate or pan with a little vegetable oil to prevent the burgers from sticking. Cook the burgers for 5–7 minutes on the first side, then flip and cook for 3 minutes more. Add a quarter of a slice of cheese to the top of each burger and cook for another 2–4 minutes, or until the cheese has melted and the burger has cooked through. If your griddle pan has a lid, you can cover the pan after you've added the cheese to help it melt.

Serve your mini burgers in the buns or pittas, with a slice of burger cheese underneath and topped with the red onion relish, a handful of shredded lettuce and whatever other condiments you like!

SUMMERY SAUSAGE ROLLS

A very traditional British snack for a very traditional British trip to the beach! These chunky sausage rolls have a few secret ingredients though – lemon zest and extra flavourings in the sausagemeat and fennel seeds on top. I won't judge you if you take a little pot of ketchup with you!

PREP: 15 minutes
COOKING: 20–25 minutes

MAKES 8

1 x 500g block of all-butter puff pastry
500g sausagemeat
finely grated zest of ½ lemon
several sprigs of thyme, leaves finely chopped (about 1 tbsp)
1 tbsp runny honey
1 tbsp Dijon mustard
1 egg, beaten with a splash of milk
plain flour, for dusting

for the tops
2 tsp fennel seeds
1 tsp coarse sea salt

Preheat the oven to 200°C/180°C fan/gas 6 and take your puff pastry out of the fridge. Line a baking tray with non-stick baking paper.

If your sausagemeat has come in sausage form, remove the meat from the casings by slitting each one open with a sharp knife and taking the meat out of each case. Add the meat to a bowl. Add the lemon zest, thyme, honey and mustard. Mix well with your hands, being sure to combine the ingredients well.

Unwrap the pastry and place on a lightly floured work surface. With a floured rolling pin, roll it out to a rectangle, about 40 x 20cm and 5mm thick. Using your hands, form the sausagemeat into one long, fat oblong and place along the bottom of your pastry, along the long edge. From the bottom, roll the log up in the pastry, sealing the join by brushing the pastry with the egg wash. Roll it gently back and forth on your work surface, so you have an evenly round oblong.

Using a clean, sharp knife, cut your log into 8 pieces, each 5cm wide, using long strokes to slice through and taking care not to press down so you don't squish the log and flatten it. Separate each slice and place on your lined baking tray, allowing a few centimetres of space around each one as they will expand in the oven. Brush the tops and any exposed pastry with the egg wash. Sprinkle the tops evenly with the fennel seeds and sea salt and place on a high shelf in the oven.

Bake for 20–25 minutes, or until the pastry is puffed up and golden brown. Remove from the oven and allow to cool for 5 minutes before removing the sausage rolls to a wire rack to cool completely. If you're taking them on a picnic, be sure they are fully cooled before packing them into a box or bag for transportation.

GREEK ORZO SALAD

This lovely colourful salad always reminds me of summer holidays. Make sure you use really juicy sweet tomatoes for maximum flavour. It actually tastes better if you let it sit in the dressing for a while, so make it a little bit in advance. You can leave out the orzo if you prefer.

PREP: 20 minutes
COOKING: 10 minutes

SERVES 4-6
as part of a picnic

250g orzo pasta, or another
 very small pasta shape
400g cherry vine tomatoes,
 quartered
1 cucumber, cut into roughly
 1cm cubes or chunks
1 red onion, thinly sliced
2 yellow, red or orange
 peppers, cut into 1cm
 chunks
50g pitted Kalamata olives,
 drained
150g feta, crumbled
2 tsp dried oregano
15g parsley leaves, chopped
finely grated zest of
 1/2 lemon
salt and black pepper

for the dressing
1 tbsp red wine vinegar
2 tsp Dijon mustard
2 tsp honey
3 tbsp olive oil

Bring a large pan of salted water to the boil over a high heat. Cook the orzo (or other pasta) for 8-10 minutes until al dente, or according to the packet instructions. Drain into a fine sieve and rinse under the cold tap for a minute to stop it from cooking. Set it to one side to drain fully.

Add the quartered tomatoes to a large mixing bowl and sprinkle with about 1 teaspoon of salt and a crack of black pepper. Toss them in the salt – this will allow them to release their juice, which makes the dressing all the more delicious.

Add the cucumber, onion, peppers and olives to the bowl with the tomatoes. Add the crumbled feta, sprinkle over the dried oregano and toss to combine.

In a small bowl, whisk the vinegar, mustard, honey and oil together and season with a little salt and pepper.

Add your cooled, drained orzo to the vegetables, pour over the vinaigrette and toss the whole lot together. Serve in a large bowl or platter, or take to the beach in a large, sealable container. Garnish with the chopped parsley and lemon zest.

HALLOUMI SKEWERS

I think I could eat grilled halloumi for every meal in the summer! It's perfect here in these easy veggie kebabs. You don't have to cook these on the barbecue of course – you could grill or griddle them at home too.

PREP: 5 minutes
COOKING: 6–8 minutes
  (on the barbecue)
  15–30 minutes (in the oven)

MAKES 2–3 big skewers
or 4–5 smaller ones

1 x 225g block of halloumi,
  cut into 2–3cm chunks
1 courgette, cut into 2–3cm
  chunks
1 red, orange or yellow
  pepper, cut into 2–3cm
  chunks
8 cherry tomatoes
2 sprigs of rosemary, leaves
  finely chopped
2 tsp sweet smoked paprika
1 tsp salt
2 tbsp olive oil
black pepper

essential equipment:
skewers

If you're using wooden skewers, soak them for 30 minutes before you use them, to ensure they don't burn over the barbecue (or in the oven).

Add the halloumi, courgette and pepper chunks to a mixing bowl with the cherry tomatoes. Add the rosemary, smoked paprika, salt, olive oil and some pepper. Toss all the ingredients together to coat.

Load your skewers by threading the ingredients on one by one. Lay your finished skewers on a plate and set to one side until you're ready to cook.

Preheat the barbecue, if you're cooking on it, and once it's nice and hot, lay the skewers over the grill, giving them some space around each. Try to control the flames so that they don't touch the skewers and burn the cheese and veg. Cook for 3–4 minutes on each side, until the tomatoes are blistered and the halloumi has browned on all sides.

(To cook them indoors, place the skewers on a baking tray and cook for 20–30 minutes in an oven preheated to 190°C/170°C fan/gas 5, turning once or twice.)

Serve alongside salads and other grilled vegetables and meat, drizzled with any of the leftover herby oil. These are also delicious with hummus and cucumber in a pitta bread.

MINI ETON MESSES

Such a cute summery pudding that you can easily transport to the beach in individual containers in your picnic hamper. If you have time, give the meringues a go... or you can just buy them from the supermarket.

PREP: 30 minutes
COOKING: 1 hour
COOLING: at least 3 hours
ASSEMBLY: 10 minutes

SERVES 6–8

for the meringues
3 egg whites (with absolutely no yolk)
150g caster sugar

for the strawberries and cream
500g strawberries
2 tbsp caster sugar
250ml double cream
1 vanilla pod (or 1 tsp vanilla bean paste)
150g Greek-style yoghurt

essential equipment:
stand mixer or electric beaters

Preheat the oven to 150°C/130°C fan/gas 2. Line a baking tray with non-stick baking paper.

Add your egg whites for the meringues to a clean, dry bowl and whisk until soft, foamy peaks form (use a stand mixer if you have one). Spoon in the sugar, one tablespoon at a time, whisking until it has all been added and the mixture is stiff, smooth and glossy. You know it's ready if you scoop a little bit out of the bowl with your finger and you can't feel the grains of sugar when you rub it gently between your finger and thumb.

Spoon the mixture onto the lined baking tray into little clouds, about 3 tbsp each. They don't need to be too tidy, because you'll be crushing them up later, but they should all be roughly the same size so that they bake evenly.

Pop the tray in the oven and cook for 1 hour, then switch off the oven heat and allow the meringues to cool inside the oven – try to resist the temptation to open the door before they are completely cool.

While the meringues are baking and cooling, wash the strawberries. Set aside a few to use as decoration, then hull and slice the rest and put them in a mixing bowl. Sprinkle over the sugar, then mix gently with a metal spoon. Leave at room temperature so the flavours can blend together.

Pour the cream into a clean mixing bowl and whip to soft peaks. Using a sharp, pointed knife, slice down the length of the vanilla pod and use the back, blunt side of the knife to scrape the tiny seeds out of the pod. (You can save the scraped pod to add to granulated sugar to make vanilla sugar, or to add to milk when making hot chocolate.) Add the seeds, or vanilla bean paste if using, to the cream and gently whip a little more to combine. Fold in the yoghurt and chill until you're ready to make the messes.

For an extra touch when serving, you can pour a little of the strawberry syrup over the Eton messes and place a strawberry on top!

PUP PARTY

Towards the end of summer, our little black pug Nala and her brother Buzz (who belongs to my boyfriend's parents) celebrate their birthday. Now, I understand not every pet owner will have the desire to celebrate their furry friend's special day, but I'm a hostess at heart, and if there is a celebration to be had, you'll bet I'll have it – and a doggy birthday is no exception. Nala is always very happy with her pressies and pupcakes (see page 126), and it's a nice excuse to get the family together too.

If you're anything like me and like to make a complete fuss of your beloved pet, then putting together a little party for them, even if that's just a couple of hours out of your day, will bring you and them heaps of joy. They only get to celebrate certain milestones, like we do, after all! We usually just get the family together and Nala and Buzz receive cards from one another (that are hilarious for the adults)

and a few dog toys, and I make them some pupcakes. We get them balloons (probably slightly excessive but I am a crazy dog lady), paper hats and party plates to eat their cakes off too. To be honest, they are mostly just interested in the dog toys and their pupcakes, but it's nice that we can all get together and talk about the love we have for our dogs... and whether or not they will throw up or poop on the carpet later that evening.

We then all have dinner together, whether that's a takeaway, a pub roast or a tapas-style evening with small dishes to pick from. One day I'm planning on doing a slightly larger doggy party where I invite all my friends who have dogs and ask them to bring their four-legged friends along with them so they can all run riot in the garden while the adults get to socialise. I'm imaging it like a scene from *Dr. Dolittle* and I cannot wait!

PUPCAKES

Every year I throw a little pup birthday party for Nala and her brother Buzz and I give them a little pupcake each to eat! They look so adorable in their hats. They always have a race to see who can finish their cake the quickest. It's usually Nala, who will then try and eat Buzz's cake.

PREP: 10 minutes
COOKING: 15-18 minutes
COOLING: at least
40 minutes

MAKES 9

2 medium carrots, coarsely
  grated (no need to peel)
1 very ripe banana
130g wholemeal flour
40g jumbo rolled oats
1¹/₂ tsp bicarbonate of soda
5 tbsp natural, unsweetened
  peanut butter (chunky or
  smooth) – make sure it's
  suitable for dogs
1 large egg
60ml vegetable oil
1 tbsp honey

for the frosting
2 x 250g tubs of cream
  cheese
6 tbsp smooth natural,
  unsweetened peanut
  butter – make sure it's
  suitable for dogs
small dog treats,
  to decorate

essential equipment:
muffin tin and paper
  cupcake cases or 18cm
  round cake tin
stand mixer or electric
  beaters

Preheat the oven to 170°C/150°C fan/gas 3¹/₂. Line a muffin tin with 9 paper cases, or grease an 18cm cake tin with a little vegetable oil.

Put the grated carrots into a mixing bowl, add the banana and mash it with a fork. Add your remaining cake ingredients and stir together with a spoon. Pour the batter into the 9 muffin cups or the cake tin.

Bake for 15-18 minutes (a little longer for the single cake), until the top is nice and golden brown, then remove from the oven and leave to cool completely.

Make your frosting by beating the cream cheese and peanut butter together in the bowl of a stand mixer, or in a bowl using electric beaters. Beat until creamy, then spoon into a piping bag fitted with a large plain or fluted nozzle. Pipe your frosting onto the tops of the pupcakes or the one larger cake. Decorate with little dog treats.

Don't forget to remove the paper cases before serving to your furry friends!

TIP
To create peanut butter stripes in the cream cheese frosting, smooth two lines of peanut butter inside your empty piping bag before filling it with the cream cheese. This looks really impressive and is so easy!

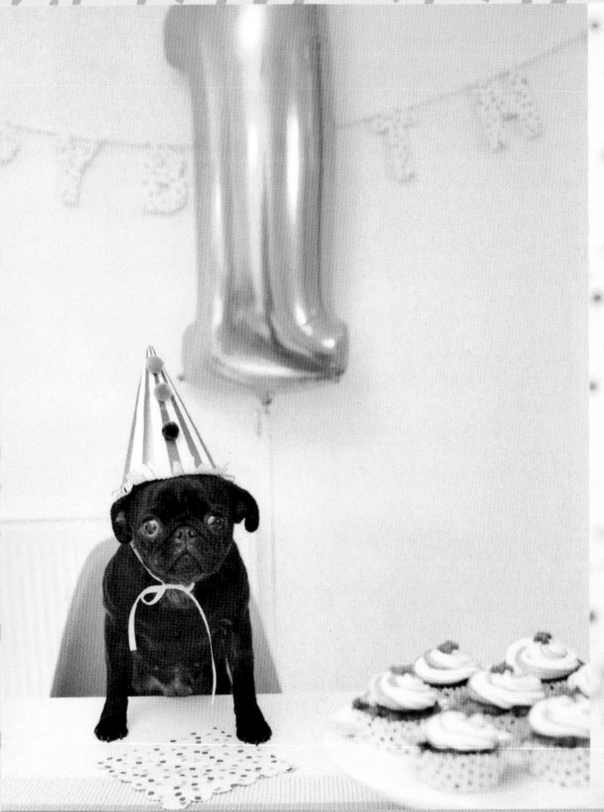

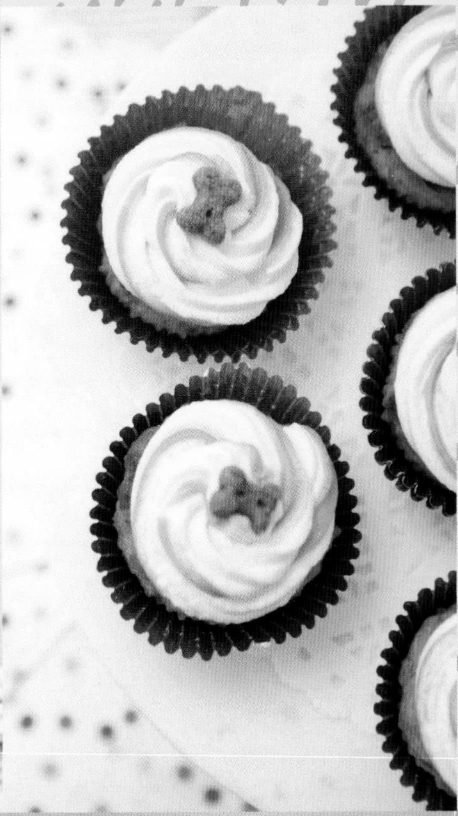

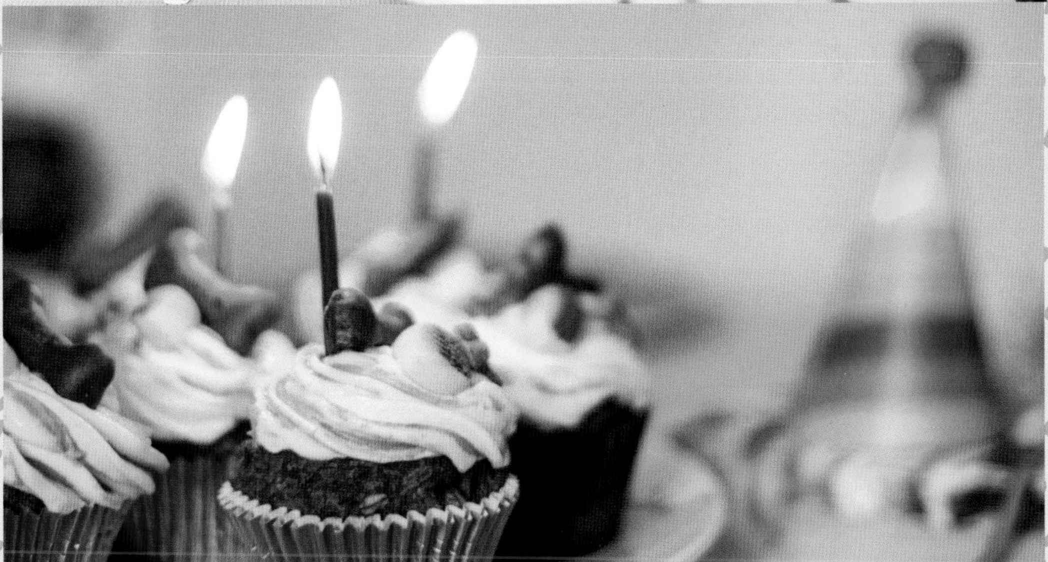

PUG PAWTY HATS

LOW EFFORT

Since a birthday isn't a birthday without a party hat, here's how to make a special *pawty* hat for your best furry friend.

You will need:

sheets of plain white card
pencil
paper scissors
washi tape in rainbow colours
small shop-bought mini pom
    pom (make sure it conforms
    to toy safety standards)
hot glue gun or double-sided
    sticky tape
ribbon to tie the hat on with

How to:

1 Using a plate or bowl (or something else circular), draw a semi-circle onto a piece of plain card. The size of this semi-circle will depend on the size of the dog's head you're making the hat for. For Nala, I drew a semi-circle that was 20cm in diameter.

2 Cut away a triangular section of the semi-circle. Imagine the semi-circle is half of a clockface – the shape you're looking for is the equivalent of between 12 o'clock and 4 o'clock.

3 Now cut a tiny semi-circle away from the top point of the hat – about 1.5cm in diameter. This will make it easier to attach the pom pom later.

4 Bring the two long straight edges of the card together to make a cone shape and check the size of the hat against your dog's head (you aren't fixing the sides together at this stage). If you need to make any adjustments to the size of the hat, now is the time to do it.

5 Using strips of coloured washi tape, decorate the card. Either carry the ends of the washi tape over to the reverse side of the card or trim the washi tape flush with the card to neaten.

6 Bring the two long straight edges of the card together again and, using double-sided sticky tape, fix the sides of the cone together.

7 Finish the hat with a small shop-bought pom pom, fixing it to the tops using a hot glue gun.

8 Tape a length of ribbon onto each side to keep the hat in place on your dog's head. Make sure all the glue is fully dry before placing on top of your dog's head!

SAFETY FIRST! Never leave your dog unattended whilst wearing the party hat and do not allow them to chew either the hat or the pom pom. When you tie the ribbon under your dog's chin, do not make the ribbon too tight.

PIZZA PARTY

On the occasion that you have friends or family coming to stay and it's a little last minute or you've had a really busy week, something I love to do instead of thinking about cooking a three-course meal (which, let's be honest, is a very rare occurance in my household) is a less formal 'pizza party'. Sometimes, pizza might mean scrolling through the local pizza places and getting some delivered, but if you want it to look like you've made at least *some* effort, making your own pizzas is a really fun and creative thing to do and can involve everyone. It also means you aren't having to juggle different dietary requirements as each person can create their perfect pizza without you having the pressure of getting it right.

Some places do amazing pre-made dough that just requires defrosting, but if you know there is a weekend coming up and you want to do this, it's really nice to make the dough yourself and you will feel a lot more accomplished. It's also VERY easy! All you really need to think about is stocking up on toppings and tomato passata base. As long as you get a nice wide variety of toppings then everyone will have something they love. See overleaf for a good basic pizza dough recipe and some suggested topping ideas. I also like to buy pre-grated cheese as this saves a lot of time. Mozzarella is the best type of cheese to use on a pizza, but I have been known to throw on a few dollops of mascarpone and this is delicious too. Alfie usually goes for the strangest concoction of toppings, including baked beans, tuna and sweetcorn…

My secret weapon is always sprinkling grated Parmesan on the crust of the pizza as it makes it that little bit more tasty!

The one thing you should do is ensure that you have enough space to all be rolling out the dough at the same time and that you have enough rolling pins – although we've had a few occasions where someone has been using a wine bottle, and that's all part of the fun! Something like this is such a relaxed and enjoyable way of hosting your friends, and we do it quite often in our house.

For pudding we will often end up making our own ice cream sundaes! See page 134 for some topping ideas. The wilder the better! The evening is usually then followed by a few gin and tonics, a good movie and a couple of board games!

PIZZA
(my fave!)

Entertaining doesn't always have to be formal or take loads of preparation. For a relaxed, easy-going evening with your close friends, a pizza party is where it's at! Here is a basic dough recipe and some delicious pizza topping combinations. You can have fun making up your own, just be careful not to overload them or you won't get a nice crispy base.

PREP: 25 minutes
RISING/PROVING TIME:
1 hour 20 minutes
COOKING: 12 minutes

MAKES 4

for the dough
450g strong white flour, plus extra for dusting
3 tsp sugar
3 tsp salt
14g dried fast-action yeast
2 tbsp olive oil, plus extra for greasing
300ml warm (not hot) water

Add the dry ingredients, including the yeast, to a large mixing bowl and make a well in the centre. Pour in the olive oil and water and mix to make a rough dough. Tip your dough out onto a well floured work surface and knead for 10–12 minutes until you have a smooth, elastic dough. (Alternatively, if you have a stand mixer with a dough hook attachment, you can do this on a low speed to knead the dough.) Shape into a ball and put in an oiled bowl. Cover the bowl with cling film and leave to rise in a warm place for an hour.

Knock back your risen dough, tip onto the floured work surface and knead for 2 minutes. Divide the dough in half, then the halves in half again to give you four balls of dough. Leave to rest on the work surface for 20 minutes, covered loosely with a clean tea towel.

Preheat the oven to 220°C/200°C fan/gas 7.

Roll or stretch each dough ball out to make a thin pizza base and pop onto floured baking sheets before topping. Remember, try not to overload your pizza (despite temptation) or you'll end up with a soggy bottom.

Cook each pizza in the oven for 10–12 minutes or until the base is golden and crisp. To make the base crisper, remove from the baking sheet and allow to sit on the shelf in the oven for the last 3–5 minutes of cooking.

pesto, chicken, tomato & feta
Spread **1–2 tbsp fresh pesto** onto your pizza base. Scatter over **50–75g shredded cooked chicken** and **4 sun-dried tomatoes** from a jar, roughly chopped. Crumble **50g feta** over the top, then drizzle with **1–2 tbsp runny honey**. Bake in the oven until the feta has browned slightly and the base is crispy. The cheese won't be melty like mozzarella.

pepperoni with chilli & honey
Spread your pizza base with **1–2 tbsp passata**, then layer **40–50g pepperoni slices**, **1 red chilli**, thinly sliced into rounds, **1 tsp dried oregano** and **50g grated mozzarella** on top. Drizzle with **1 tbsp runny honey** as soon as it comes out of the oven.

grilled vegetable & artichoke
Spread **1–2 tbsp passata** over the pizza base, then top with **several slices of grilled courgette or aubergine**, **4–5 pieces of artichoke heart from a jar**, cut into large chunks and **50g grated mozzarella**. Bake in the oven, then tear **a few basil leaves** over the top when it comes out of the oven. If you like, drizzle with a little bit of **balsamic glaze** (see page 52 for homemade).

To **grill courgette or aubergine**, trim a courgette or aubergine and slice lengthways, brush the slices with a little olive oil, season with salt and pepper and cook under the grill, on a hot barbecue or in a griddle pan until soft with charred grill marks on both sides for 5–10 minutes in total. Allow to cool before using to top your pizza.

ICE CREAM SUNDAE BAR

Much like the pizza party on the previous page, doing something like this for a dessert with friends is so much fun and very customisable! It's all about the toppings!! Go crazy and have loads of bowls of different sprinkles, mini doughnuts, sweets and syrups on your table and then pile them all up on top of your ice cream. Alternatively, you could go down the healthy route and use frozen yoghurt, fruit and nuts.

PREP: 5-10 minutes

SERVES 6-8

1 litre ice cream, sorbet, frozen yoghurt or dairy-free alternative (choose your very favourite flavours and mix it up by buying 2, or even 3, smaller tubs of different flavours)

Take your ice cream out of the freezer for 5-10 minutes before serving, to allow it to soften just a little bit. Prepare and serve your chosen toppings in individual bowls, jars or glasses. Warm any sauces you'd like according to the packet instructions and pour them into jugs, or just serve at room temperature.

Serve 2 or 3 scoops per person, then let loose and create indulgent masterpieces.

If you're in the mood to create freakshake chaos, add 2 scoops of your chosen ice cream flavour to a blender and top with the milk, and the cocoa powder if you're going chocolatey. Blitz it together to create a really thick shake. Pour it out into a large glass (the bigger the better) and add another scoop or two of ice cream before going completely mad with toppings and sauces. Again, the bigger the better – go for cookies, sweets, chocolate bars, whipped cream, waffles, macarons, lots and lots of sauce, sprinkles and a cherry to top it all off – the sky (and your sweet tooth) is the limit. Serve with a long spoon and a thick drinking straw.

topping ideas
toasted chopped hazelnuts
flaked toasted almonds
salted roasted peanuts
toasted coconut flakes
fresh berries (strawberries, raspberries or blueberries), sliced or cut up
fresh soft fruit (mango, peaches, nectarines or bananas), sliced or cut up
mini doughnuts or mini Belgian waffles
Bourbon biscuits, custard creams or Oreos
party rings, pretzels
wafer rolls, caramel wafers
mini flapjack or millionaire shortbread bites
chocolate brownies, chopped into chunks
mini chocolate bars, chopped
Maltesers, Smarties, M&Ms
Mint Cremes
chocolate buttons or chocolate chips
sprinkles, popping candy, mini marshmallows
profiteroles
maraschino cherries
macarons

sauce suggestions
squirty cream or whipped double cream
fudge sauce, warmed
chocolate sauce, warmed
strawberry syrup
toffee sauce
Nutella
honey, golden syrup or maple syrup
yoghurt
fruit coulis

if you'd like to make a freakshake
100ml milk per person
2 tsp unsweetened cocoa powder (optional)

TIP
To embellish the glass, before adding your sundae, dribble melted chocolate along the rim and cover in sprinkles.

TIP

To make your ice cream masterpiece more impressive and to provide a bit of height, create a sweet treat skewer to insert into the glass!

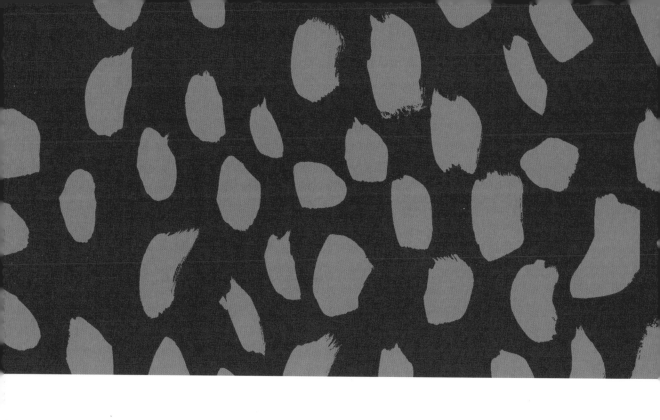

Aut

umn

Collect some conkers, light the fire and snuggle up under a blanket: this is the time of year when you want to get cosy and start preparing for the darker, colder months ahead. The evening light is warm and orange and so are the leaves on the trees and crunching beneath feet on evening walks, with the lingering smell of burning bonfires in the air. After rounding up the summer months, head filled with happy sun-filled memories, autumn is definitely my favourite season of the year. I am like a little mouse, and am truly my most relaxed and happy next to a crackling fire in the evening and under a blanket on the sofa, enjoying the fading autumn light, with a hot chocolate and the candles lit. I find the lovely glow of dusk, combined with the slight chill in the air, a perfect combination.

As the days turn colder and the nights begin to get longer, I like to add a few autumnal home touches too, including far too many pumpkin spice candles, as well as thicker bedding and lots of soft throws beside the sofa. I also have some autumnal decorations that I like to scatter through my home, including an autumn leaf wreath (see page 164 for how to make your own), pine cones galore collected on many autumn walks, and checked flannel everything. I don't believe seasonal displays are only for Christmas, and there is something really lovely about collecting conkers and different orange-toned leaves to scatter around your table centrepiece or along your fireplace mantel. I'm also a huge fan of the little munchkin pumpkins and squashes you can buy in supermarkets!

The start of the colder months also means having more baths. Whereas I tend to be a lot more of a shower girl in the hotter months, I find baths very relaxing during the colder ones. There really is nothing more indulgent than a deep bubbly bath with lots of candles.

Autumn also offers endless hosting possibilities, with events such as Halloween and Bonfire Night, where you can get really creative and go a little more crazy with your party ideas. Halloween for me is one of the best excuses

> I am truly my most relaxed and happy next to a crackling fire in the evening and under a blanket on the sofa.

to throw a party. I've always loved fancy dress but as an adult you're a little more limited on times during the year when you can get dressed up – with Halloween, it's a given! The days around Bonfire Night are a time when I'm constantly smiling up at the sky, watching multiple firework displays happening all around. Is there really anything more spectacular?

Another thing I love to do at this time of year is go pumpkin picking with friends (although always wanting the biggest, roundest pumpkin does require rolling it to the car). Getting them home and deciding how you want to decorate them is also part of the fun! (See page 151 for my pumpkin painting project.)

Food at this time of the year is much more comforting and hearty, with delicious soups, jacket potatoes and the never-ending hunt for the perfect pub roast dinner on a Sunday (I am still on my quest). I also love this time of year for baking, as the spices start to make an appearance – and autumn in my house will never go by without an abundance of pumpkin spice cupcakes to go around! (See my recipe on page 174.) It's also the season of pies – chicken pies, blackberry and apple pies, plum pies… basically every pie you can think of! Talking of blackberries, autumn is the season of foraging. Growing up we always used to go out and pick blackberries so that Mum could bake them in a pie or a crumble, arriving back home with purple lips and fingertips. If you don't have somewhere near you where you can pick your own, head to a local farmers' market instead and stock up on the colourful seasonal bounty.

Autumn in my house will never go by without an abundance of pumpkin spice cupcakes!

AUTUMN TO-DO LIST

○ Change up your bedding: bring out the flannels and up the duvet tog.

○ Stock up on wood and kindling if you have a fire.

○ Scatter throws and blankets around your bedroom and living room.

○ Bring out your autumnal scented candles. Pumpkin spice and woody scents are my favourite!

○ Collect conkers and leaves on your walks for decorating the house or using in crafts.

○ Go on walks through local woods or National Trust nature reserves (see page 159).

○ Go pumpkin picking and then decorate them! (See page 151 for ideas)

○ Create a Halloween playlist.

○ Pick your Halloween costume (see page 146 for ideas).

○ Have a Halloween movie night (see page 144).

○ Stock up on sparklers.

○ Get out your woolly hats and scarves.

○ Attend a local fireworks display.

○ Drink all the chai and pumpkin spice lattes (see page 177).

○ Visit a local farmers' market for the best autumnal produce.

○ Make toffee apples and s'mores.

○ Make a hedgehog house.

○ Make hot, spiced cider.

○ Stock up on every flavour of hot chocolate and mini marshmallows.

○ Start internally getting excited for Christmas (it's still too early for most people).

HALLOWEEN

I must admit, this is one of my favourite times of year for parties and get-togethers. I absolutely love Halloween, and although here in the UK it's not taken as seriously as it is in other parts of the world, I throw everything into it and give it my absolute all. I'm a big horror movie fan and love having friends over, turning out the lights, snuggling under blankets and jumping out of our skin! You can of course watch horror movies all year round, but Halloween is the perfect time to whip out the extra spooky ones or some of the classics.

Must-watch films for Halloween:

Casper
Hocus Pocus
Labyrinth
The Nightmare Before Christmas
Practical Magic
Edward Scissorhands
Get Out
Insidious
Paranormal Activity
Sinister
Scream
The Conjuring
The Ring

If you want to make the most of Halloween, why not turn it into more of a party? Crack out the music, the snacks and, the best part... the costumes. This can be done with a guest list that is either big or small, depending on how much space you want to occupy and how much food you want to supply. One thing to bear in mind, though, is that when the guest list becomes a lot bigger, being able to seat everyone to watch a movie together will also be more difficult. You may have to scrap that element of the night and instead make it more of a party and less of a movie night.

As adults, I know you can't go trick-or-treating anymore but that doesn't mean you can't decorate the pathway up to your front door and your entrance way, and have a bowl of Halloween-themed sweets for your guests. One year, I lined my porch steps with carved pumpkins, tea lights and fake cobwebs and it was magical.

Cobwebs are an absolute must for any Halloween shindig. They are so cheap and you can pick them up in most supermarkets and party shops around this time of the year. They create a huge impact and can turn a really basic space into a creepy, abandoned room in minutes. If you are a bit nervous about throwing a house party with quite a lot of guests, the one time of year that would be perfect to give it a shot is Halloween because you can drape old sheets and rags over all your carpets and furniture and it will just look like part of the creepy decor! If anything is spilt, it won't matter as much.

I remember when I was young my mum and dad threw a Halloween party in our house for all their friends, and it looked like so much fun. Mum hung black and orange crepe tissue from the ceilings, put cobwebs absolutely everywhere and had plastic bats and rats hanging at head height to frighten people as they walked from room to room. The lights were dimmed and everything was lit with candles and it felt so spooky and cosy. Everyone had to dress up in Halloween costumes too, which made for some great laughs and photographs! Being able to do this in my own home now makes me so happy. I feel like it's the one time of the year you can get seriously creative with your hair, make-up and costume, without having to worry at all about what you look like, because the worse... the better.

Mum's tip

If you have reed diffusers,
just before guests arrive,
turn over the reeds to
give them maximum
scent!

LAST-MINUTE COSTUME IDEAS WITH A BIT MORE CREATIVITY (NO WITCHES HATS OR CAT WHISKERS ALLOWED):

Jareth from *Labyrinth*. This was my Halloween costume of choice last year, and it was extremely last minute. I spotted an 80s-style blonde wig in the costume shop and immediately thought of Jareth the Goblin King. I then grabbed a frilly shirt, bought an old waistcoat from a vintage shop and dug out a pair of grey leggings. Some over-the-knee boots, a dash of make-up and a sock down the pants later... and I was ready!

Jigsaw from the *Saw* movies. This one is mostly make-up focused, as costume-wise all you need is a white shirt, black blazer, black trousers or skirt and a little red dickie bow. The face paint colours are pretty standard too – only red, white and black, which come in many of the more basic sets you can buy. Definitely something a little more fun than those cat whiskers!

Eleven from *Stranger Things*. A blonde wig, a blue bomber jacket, a pink dress, some sport knee socks and some white plimsolls and you're pretty much good to go. If you can get yourself a box of Eggos, though, you're an A+ costume student.

Samara from *The Ring*. This really is SUPER easy. Make your hair greasy and backcombed (or you know... don't wash it for a week) or grab yourself a long brown wig and mess it up, pull it over your face and pick up a white nightie that you can cut a few holes in and mess up. Dab some bruises on your arms and legs using a sponge and some black and purple body paint, make your face as ghostly white as possible and there you have it... the creepy girl from *The Ring*.

The Sanderson sisters from *Hocus Pocus*. This one is fun to do with two friends and is a fun twist on a more basic witch's outfit. Perfecting the ultimate period witch's outfit is going to be acomplished by scouring your local vintage and charity shops! You will need to assign a colour to each person – one wears purple, one wears green and the other wears burgundy. Layer different items of clothing, securing with belts and ribbons – and get a bit wacky and creative with the hair! It's also just really fun to do this with friends and feel like a fierce trio all evening.

Pet costumes! You might not be the sort of person whose love of costumes extends to their pets, but having a small dog myself, it's all too fun and entertaining (thankfully, she loves it). She's quite accustomed to a chunky knit jumper throughout the colder months, but Halloween is definitely when she goes to town with her costume choices! Two of her favourites being her scorpion and spider outfits.

THE FOOD

When it comes to Halloween food at parties, a big old buffet that people can help themselves to is probably your best bet. You can make the food yourself or buy it in, depending on how great you are in the kitchen – or do a bit of both. It's nice to make at least a few Halloween treats though, like cupcakes, meringues or biscuits, as these are super simple and so delicious (see pages 154–157 for my spooky Halloween recipes).

There are also some amazing cake decorations, cake toppers and cupcake cases around this time of the year, so you are sure to find something that would look amazing on your Halloween food display. I like to lay out a huge table with nibbles and sweet treats, and a pile of plates for people to help themselves or come back to before sitting down to watch the scary

TIP

Leave face wipes out for guests who start to rub their hands on their faces or forget they have make-up all over them as the evening draws on. It's better to have these to hand than to be scrubbing black fingerprints off your white walls the next day!

Mum's tip

If you have quite a big number of guests coming, plug in some phone chargers around the house so people aren't coming to ask you where they can find one.

movie. A big part of laying out a table for a party or themed occasion is really setting the scene. Using Halloween-themed bowls, dishes and plates instead of serving food in their cartons or containers makes everything look so much more spectacular. I also like to keep some grab bags available so people can take home any leftover haul! See how to make my glow-in-the-dark grab bags on page 152.

One year, I found a big silver dish with bird feet and a skeleton that stands tall with two bowls over his shoulders. It's great for snacks! These kinds of items don't have to be expensive – shops like Home Bargains, HomeSense, TK Maxx and even most supermarkets will have lots of choice. If you're putting together a display table, then I find that it's visually very appealing to have things at different heights and served on different textures. I have a great black lace tablecloth that I put down and then arrange some spooky candelabras and little pumpkins and squashes in between the dishes and bowls. You can find my Halloween pumpkin painting project – a prettier twist on the usual pumpkin carving idea – on page 151.

There really is no limit when it comes to Halloween: more is more and it's hard to go overboard. If anything, it's easier to *under*-do it and then it doesn't feel very spooky at all. If you don't have a lot of decorations, think about decorating just one room of the house for maximum impact, rather than having just a few bits and pieces scattered all over the house.

There really is no limit when it comes to Halloween: more is more and it's hard to go overboard.

DECORATIVE PUMPKINS

As well as carving a big orange pumpkin this year, why not decorate some of the smaller squashes, including pumpkins and gourds? I like to create a display using lots of squashes in all different sizes, painting them first in white or black, then adding copper accents.

You will need:

autumn squashes
newspaper
sealant spray (optional)
acrylic spray paint in black and white
metallic copper acrylic paint
paintbrush

How to:

1 Wash the skin of the squash really well to remove any dirt and grease, and leave it to dry thoroughly, especially the stem – if this stays wet it can cause the squash to rot.

2 If you want to prolong the life of your painted squash, you can spray the squash all over with sealant. Do this somewhere with plenty of ventilation and over some sheets of newspaper. This will also give you a better surface for painting, as the paint will stick more easily. If using, spray a liberal coating of sealant all over the squash and leave to dry thoroughly.

3 To spray your entire squash in a single colour, lay down sheets of newspaper to protect your work surface (I did this outside!). To make sure that the painted squash didn't stick on the newspaper, I placed my squash on a wire cooling rack. Then to make sure I contained the spray paint, I placed an opened-up cardboard box behind the squash. Using a can of acrylic spray paint, carefully cover the entire surface of the squash. Leave it to dry thoroughly. If necessary, spray the squash again with a second coat of paint to get a smooth, evenly coloured surface. You will probably need to leave it overnight to dry properly.

4 Once the base coat of colour is dry, use the metallic copper acrylic paint and a paintbrush to add any highlights to the squash.

TIP

When choosing your squash, check it has no blemishes or rotting areas, especially around the stem and base. Also check that the squash sits flat and does not roll around.

HALLOWEEN GRAB BAGS

Spooky grab bags are perfect to give any visiting ghouls a treat at Halloween. You can stencil plain paper bags with any design you like. I am obsessed with skulls, but you can obviously use whatever other creepy things associated with Halloween you like best! Or even just skip that part and go straight for a splat of blood!

You will need:

pencil
A4 sheets of black card
paper scissors or scalpel
newspaper
small brown paper party
  bags with a flat base
sticky tape
Blutack
white acrylic spray paint
glow-in-the-dark acrylic
  paint (optional)
crimson red acrylic ink with
  a dropper
paintbrush
paperclips or small pegs

To make the glow-in-the-dark skull design:

1 To make your skull stencil, draw your skull shape onto a piece of black card. I found an image online, printed it and cut it out and then drew around that. I then drew in the details (the eye and nose sockets and the teeth) freehand.

2 Using paper scissors or a scalpel, very carefully cut along the pencil lines to leave a skull-shaped hole in the centre of the black card. Cut out the eye and nose sockets and set aside the black card skull to use later.

3 In a well ventilated space, lay down sheets of newspaper to protect your work surface. Take a party bag and place it on the newspaper. Position your skull stencil on top of the party bag and tape down the edges to the newspaper to hold the stencil in place. Carefully position the eye and nose socket pieces and hold them in place with tiny pieces of Blutack. Following the instructions on the can, spray the stencil evenly with spray paint and then leave to dry for a few minutes.

4 Carefully remove the stencil and cut-out eye and nose pieces from the party bag, taking care not to smudge the paint. Set aside to dry thoroughly. Once dry, you can add extra highlights to the white skull, using glow-in-the-dark acrylic paint with a paintbrush.

5 Repeat the above steps, reusing the stencil, to paint as many party bags as you need. (It is a good idea to let the stencil dry out a little between each spraying, so that the painted skulls all have nice crisp edges.)

To make the blood splats and black skull design:

6 Take a party bag and place it on the newspaper. Using the dropper in the ink bottle, drip drops of crimson red ink onto the bag. I did this carefully from the height of about one metre to get a decent splat! Leave to dry thoroughly.

To finish the bags:

7 Once all the bags are dry, fill your party bags with sweet Halloween treats, then fold over the top of the bags to enclose. Use a paperclip to attach the cut-out black skull to one of the blood-splat bags. For all the other bags, cut more shapes from black card – bats, spiders, ravens, whatever you like – and attach them to paperclips or small pegs to use as fasteners.

TIP

If you don't want to cut more shapes from card, for an alternative closure, make two holes in the folded-over top of the bag using a hole punch. Thread a short length of twine or thin ribbon through these holes, from the back to the front. Tie the twine or ribbon into a neat bow.

RICE KRISPIE PUMPKINS

These are so easy to make and they taste amazing. They're based on the idea of those chocolate Rice Krispies cakes we used to make at school – but with an autumn twist! (You can see a photograph of these as part of the Halloween display on pages 148–149.)

PREP: 10 minutes
SETTING: 30 minutes
DECORATING: 20 minutes

MAKES 18

50g unsalted butter, plus extra for greasing
300g marshmallows
1 tsp ground cinnamon
$\frac{1}{2}$ tsp ground nutmeg
$\frac{1}{4}$ tsp ground ginger
a pinch of salt
orange gel food colouring
200g Rice Krispies, or other puffed rice cereal
black and/or green ready-rolled fondant icing
icing sugar, for dusting

In a medium saucepan, melt the butter and marshmallows together over a medium heat, stirring often with a spoon.

Meanwhile, combine the spices and salt in a small bowl. Just before the marshmallows have completely melted, add the spices and a generous squeeze of orange gel to the pan. Keep stirring to ensure the colour and spices are evenly incorporated, adding more colouring if you'd like a vibrant finish.

Once the marshmallows are completely melted and the mixture is a nice warm orange colour, remove from the heat and tip in the Rice Krispies. Stir with a spoon to completely coat the cereal in the sticky, melted marshmallow. Allow to cool for just a few minutes then, while still warm, form into balls: rub your clean hands with butter, then roll a small handful of mixture into a ball. Flatten it a little bit to make it into a pumpkin shape, then place on a baking tray. Rub your hands with a little more butter and repeat the process with the rest of the mixture to make about 18 pumpkins.

Pop the pumpkins into the fridge for at least 30 minutes to allow them to set.

While your pumpkins are chilling, roll out the black fondant icing on a work surface dusted with icing sugar until quite thin, about 2.5mm thick. Using a small, sharp knife, cut 36 tiny triangles and 18 jack o' lantern mouths – they could be crescents, circles, toothy smiles or a combination; it's your chance to be creative. Roll 18 little 'stalks' from the green fondant icing – make a long, thin log and cut it into 18 pieces. (You can also use all black fondant icing or all green fondant icing for the decorations if you prefer.)

Once the pumpkins are firm, remove them from the fridge and, gently dampening the back of the icing shapes with a wet finger, stick two triangle eyes and a fun mouth shape onto each pumpkin. Top with a fondant stalk and serve at room temperature.

MERINGUE GHOSTS

These friendly little spirits will brighten up any Halloween display. You can choose what faces to decorate them with – these cheery chaps won't be scaring anyone! (You can see a photograph of these as part of the Halloween display on pages 148–149.)

PREP: 30 minutes
COOKING: 1 hour
COOLING: at least
  3 hours

MAKES 15–20

3 egg whites (with
  absolutely no yolk)
150g caster sugar
1 tube of black writing
  icing or black edible
  icing pen

essential equipment:
stand mixer or electric
  beaters
a piping bag fitted with a
  large plain nozzle

Preheat the oven to 150°C/130°C fan/gas 2 and line a baking tray with non-stick baking paper.

Add the egg whites to a clean, dry bowl and whisk with electric beaters until soft, foamy peaks form (use a stand mixer if you have one). Spoon in the sugar, one tablespoon at a time, whisking until it has all been added and the mixture is stiff, smooth and glossy. You know it's ready if you scoop a little bit out of the bowl with your finger and you can't feel the grains of sugar when you rub it gently between your finger and thumb.

Spoon the meringue mixture into a large piping bag fitted with a large plain nozzle. Pipe the meringue into little ghost shapes by starting with a wider, circular bottom and spiralling up to a pointed head.

Cook in the oven for 1 hour, then switch off the oven heat and allow the meringues to cool inside the oven – try to resist the temptation to open the door before they are completely cool.

When the ghosts are cool, use the black writing icing or black edible icing pen to create little spooky faces on each one. You could also serve them with a red raspberry coulis to dip them in.

SPOOKY CHOCOLATE SKELETON BISCUITS

These little skeleton biscuits are not only delicious, but bring your Halloween table to life... or death!

PREP: 20 minutes
COOLING: 30 minutes
 for the dough, plus 30–45
 minutes for the biscuits
COOKING: 10–12 minutes
 per batch

MAKES about 24,
 depending on the size
 of your cutter

250g butter, softened
140g icing sugar
2 tsp vanilla extract
1 egg yolk
300g plain flour
50g cocoa powder
1 tube of ready-made white
 writing icing (or 1 quantity
 of icing from Easter
 biscuits on page 26)

essential equipment:
person and/or bone-shaped
 biscuit cutters
piping bag fitted with a fine
 nozzle (or just snip a very
 small hole at the end of
 your piping bag)

Using a spoon or a mixer, beat together the butter, icing sugar, vanilla and egg yolk in a bowl, creaming the mixture together until well combined. Sift the flour and cocoa powder together into a separate bowl, then add it to the butter mixture a little at a time until it has all been added. The dough will look quite crumbly and dry, but press it together into a ball with your hands and wrap in cling film. Chill it in the fridge for around 30 minutes.

Preheat the oven to 190°C/170°C fan/gas 5 and line a baking tray with non-stick baking paper.

Cut two large pieces of baking paper and lay one on your work surface. Place half the dough on it, then lay the second piece of baking paper on top and, using a rolling pin, roll out the dough between the two layers of paper to a thickness of about 5mm.

Peel back the top layer of baking paper. Choose a gingerbread person and/or a bone-shaped cookie cutter and cut out your cookies, placing them on the lined baking tray as you go. If they stick a little bit to the paper underneath, use a metal spatula or thin knife to ease them off. Re-roll the dough to use it all up, and use the second half of dough to cut out more. Bake in batches if you don't have multiple baking trays. If you find that the dough is becoming too soft and warm, pop it into the fridge for a few minutes before re-rolling.

Bake each batch for 10–12 minutes, then remove from the oven and allow to cool on the tray for a few minutes before removing to a wire rack to cool completely.

Place the icing in a piping bag fitted with a fine nozzle, or snip the end off your icing bag or sandwich bag. When your cookies are cool, decorate them by drawing on little bones and skeletons with the icing.

AUTUMN WALK

Autumn is definitely one of the most beautiful times of the year to go exploring outdoors, with crisp leaves beneath your feet and conkers scattered across the road. The air feels really fresh and the golden sunsets are some of the best all year. As I've mentioned already when talking about the spring walk (see pages 46–47), I love putting on my boots, popping Nala's harness and lead on her and getting outside. I find it really motivating and a lovely start to the day or end to the week.

Some Sundays, when we have had family or friends round, we will make a walk a priority, and if you've had people to stay over the weekend, it's a nice way to get out of the house for a bit and to show them a snapshot of where you live. You might want to tie this in with a roast dinner at a local pub that you know they'd like, or you can sort out something delicious to eat when you get back, like a steaming bowl of tomato and ginger soup and a cheese toastie (see page 160). What could be better? Or even just a big mug of tea and some biscuits to warm up with in front of the fire.

If your walk is going to be a bit longer, it's a good idea to take something with you, like a flask of hot chocolate or something equally warming.

On returning to the house, this is where your evening activity comes in and we usually all decide on our favourite autumn movie (which will most likely star Meg Ryan).

Remember though, that it's not really about where your walk takes you or how beautiful it might be outside or what you might eat, or even what movie you have on in the evening, it's about creating a special atmosphere so that you can all look back on it and remember it fondly. For me, some of my best memories of all the seasons are of being outside and going on those walks.

Essential autumn watching...

Good Will Hunting
When Harry Met Sally
You've Got Mail
Sleepless in Seattle
Any Harry Potter movie!
Moulin Rouge
About Time
Dead Poets Society
Gilmore Girls
Sleepy Hollow

TOMATO & GINGER SOUP WITH TOASTIES

After a walk in the cold fresh air, I always come back ravenous. You can't beat tomato soup and cheese toasties on days like that! Make the soup before you head out, so you just have to reheat it when you get home.

PREP: 15 minutes
COOKING: 1 hour

SERVES 4

750g cherry tomatoes, halved
3 tbsp olive oil
1 red onion, chopped
2 garlic cloves, chopped
1 thumb-sized piece of fresh ginger, peeled and chopped
1 x 400g tin of chopped tomatoes
750ml vegetable stock
salt and black pepper

for the toasties
8 slices of your favourite bread
200–400g medium Cheddar, depending on the size of your bread slices, sliced about 5mm thick
unsalted butter, for spreading
fresh thyme, to garnish

essential equipment:
a hand-held blender or jug blender

Begin by making the soup. Preheat the oven to 180°C/160°C fan/gas 4. Put the cherry tomatoes into a large roasting dish, ideally ceramic. You're not looking for them to be in a single layer, more of a pile. Drizzle with 2 tablespoons of the olive oil and season generously with salt and pepper. Toss the tomatoes in the oil and seasoning and roast in the oven for 35 minutes, until they have released their juice and the tomatoes on the top have blistered, roasted skins.

Meanwhile, heat the remaining tablespoon of olive oil in a large, heavy-based pan over a medium-high heat. Add the onion, garlic and ginger and cook for 8–10 minutes until the onion is soft and the ginger is fragrant. Tip the tinned tomatoes into the pan and stir to combine, then cook for 5–7 minutes, to bring to a simmer and thicken a little.

Remove your cherry tomatoes from the oven and tip them into the pan. Add the stock and stir gently to combine. Allow this to simmer over a medium-low heat for 8–10 minutes, then remove from the heat and use a hand-held blender to blitz the soup until smooth. (If you don't have a hand blender, you can use a regular jug blender, but allow the soup mixture to cool for 20 minutes before blending.) Pour the soup through a fine-mesh sieve to remove the tomato seeds and return it to the pan. If you're eating it straight away, return the heat to low to warm the soup through. If not, you can cool the soup to reheat later.

To make the toasties, place an even layer of cheese over 4 of the slices of bread – you want the cheese to cover the whole surface of the slice without overlapping. Top the cheese with the second slice of bread and spread the outside faces of each sandwich with butter.

Heat a large frying pan over a medium-low heat and place the sandwiches in it. If you don't have enough space in one pan, use a second one or cook the sandwiches in batches. Allow the sandwiches to sit, undisturbed for 5–7 minutes. Check to see that the bread is browning, then carefully flip over and toast on the other side for another 5–7 minutes, pressing the tops of the sandwiches gently with a spatula as the cheese melts.

Serve the soup hot, with a toastie on the side, garnished with thyme, ready for dipping.

SHAKSHUKA

This is a great recipe to have in your repertoire as it mostly uses ingredients you probably already have in your cupboards – tinned tomatoes and eggs! It's perfect after a cold walk and it's really easy to size up – it also makes a great brunch.

PREP: 5 minutes
COOKING: 50 minutes

SERVES 4

2 tbsp olive oil
1 onion, chopped
2 garlic cloves, chopped
1 green pepper, cut into
   2-3cm chunks
1 red pepper, cut into
   2-3cm chunks
2 tsp sweet smoked
   paprika
1 tsp ground cumin
2 x 400g tins of
   chopped tomatoes
2 tsp caster sugar or
   honey
8 eggs
15g fresh parsley, leaves
   roughly chopped
salt and black pepper
4 slices of sourdough
   bread, toasted, to
   serve

Heat the oil in a large frying pan (that has a lid) over a medium-high heat. Cook the onion and garlic, stirring frequently, for about 5 minutes, to start them softening, then add the peppers to the pan and cook until soft, about 5 minutes. Add the spices and cook for 1-2 minutes more before adding the tinned tomatoes and the sugar or honey. Stir to combine, then reduce the heat to medium-low and simmer for 20-30 minutes to allow the sauce to thicken. Taste and season with salt and pepper.

Make 8 little wells in the sauce (if your pan isn't big enough to make 8, tip half the sauce into a second frying pan so you can cook all the eggs at once). One by one, crack the eggs into a small bowl, then tip one into each well. Cover the pan, turn the heat to low and let the eggs cook in the sauce for 10-12 minutes, or until the whites have set but the yolks are still runny or cooked to your liking.

Scatter the parsley over the top, before bringing the whole thing to the table to serve with the sourdough toast.

AUTUMN LEAF WREATH

While out dog walking, I often pick up leaves and acorns and bring them home! Real leaves tend to lose their colour and become brittle and fragile, though, so I like to use a natural twig wreath decorated with fabric leaves, which allows me to hold on to the colours of autumn for as long as I like and bring out every year!

You will need:

natural twig, rattan or wicker wreath
selection of fabric leaves
selection of faux acorns, pine cones
  and berries (optional)
hot glue gun
twine or ribbon for hanging the wreath

How to:

1 Before fixing any leaves to the wreath, lay them all out, mixing up the colours and shapes until you find an arrangement that you are happy with. You can either leave the top half of the twig wreath exposed – I love its rustic look – or you can cover all the way around. Mix up the orange, yellow, green and soft brown leaves so they are nicely blended. If you like, you can add a few clusters of berries, pine cones or acorns.

2 Using a hot glue gun, fix the leaves, berries and acorns to the wreath. Just a small dab of glue on the back of each leaf will be enough to secure it to the wreath. If you find it easier, you can glue the leaves together in clusters, layering a few leaves on top of one another, and then fix the leaf cluster to the wreath.

3 Hang the wreath in place using ribbon or twine, or place it in the middle of the table to use as a centrepiece with a candle in the middle.

BONFIRE NIGHT

Bonfire Night is one of those occasions that truly encapsulates everything I love about autumn: the smell of bonfires crackling away, the comforting food and drink, and everyone huddling together under blankets, coats, scarves and woolly hats to watch a firework display or write their name in a sparkler. It feels magical, and a proper celebratory start to the more wintry months ahead.

Bonfire Night is the perfect end to summer and it makes me that little bit more excited for the wintry events to begin.

Whether you plan to meet friends or family at a local firework display or will be hosting your own, there are certainly things you can do to make the most of it. If you're having your own firework party, you'll need a fairly large open garden space so you have the room to set off the fireworks. Before you start planning, make sure that it's safe to have fireworks where you are and assign a single person who will be in charge of lighting them.

I'm actually a little terrified of fireworks – I don't like that they can be so unpredictable – so watching them from afar is usually something I prefer to do. Some years, Alfie and I have just watched them from our open bedroom window as they've set off in various different areas around us. If you live on a hill or next to a recreation ground, you have the advantage of a free display! Other years, we've jumped in the car in our pyjamas and driven around until we've found the perfect spot to sit and watch them. What I really mean is, you don't need to be at a huge display or even put on your own to enjoy the night. And it goes without saying really that if you have pets, you need to bear them in mind. Nala doesn't like fireworks very much, so we don't usually like to leave her alone the days around Bonfire Night.

One of my favourite ways to enjoy the night is to invite a few friends round for some food and drinks in the garden. I'll set up the fire pit instead of a bonfire and have wooden crates for everyone to sit on, with a big pile of blankets for people to wrap themselves up in later. (If you do go for a bonfire, remember not to build it in advance, as hibernating hedgehogs will be attracted to it.) Cook up something really cosy like baked potatoes and a big pot of chilli – don't forget all the extras like sour cream and cheese – or maybe go for an impressive mash mountain! See pages 170–177 for my favourite Bonfire Night recipes, including pumpkin spice cupcakes and chai lattes for after dinner. Definitely don't forget the sparklers, and marshmallows for toasting over the fire!

MASH MOUNTAIN

This is a really basic meal, but it's a crowd-pleaser and a staple in our family! My dad always made the most epic mashed potatoes and it's something everyone should be able to whip up on cosy nights in!

PREP: 10 minutes
COOKING: 40 minutes

SERVES 6

2 tsp vegetable oil, for greasing
12–18 sausages, depending on how hungry you are
salt and black pepper

for the gravy
25g butter
4 onions, thinly sliced
2 tsp soft brown sugar
1 ½ tbsp plain flour
750ml vegetable or beef stock
salt and black pepper

for the mash
1.5kg Maris Piper potatoes, peeled and cut into halves or quarters
75g butter
50ml milk (optional)
salt and black pepper

Preheat the oven to 180°C/160°C fan/gas 4 and grease a baking dish or tray with the vegetable oil.

While the oven is heating up, begin the gravy. Melt the butter in a saucepan, then add the onions, sprinkle over the sugar and cook over a medium heat for 20–30 minutes, stirring frequently, until soft and caramelised.

Meanwhile, add your sausages to the oiled baking dish and cook in the oven for 25–30 minutes, turning once halfway through cooking.

Sprinkle the flour over the caramelised onions and stir to combine. Slowly add the stock, stirring all the time to avoid lumps. Season well with salt and pepper, then let the gravy simmer for 10–15 minutes to allow it to thicken slightly and develop in flavour.

Add the prepared potatoes to a large saucepan and cover with cold water. Add a generous pinch of salt and bring to the boil. Cook for 15 minutes, or until tender but still firm and not completely mushy. Tip into a colander and let them drain well and dry for a few minutes, then return the drained potatoes to the saucepan and add the butter. Mash well and, if you like your mash a little less thick, add the milk, a tablespoon or two at a time, and whip the potatoes with a spoon to make them creamier. Season well with salt and pepper.

Compose your mash mountain by tipping all the mash out onto a serving platter and, with a spoon, sculpting it into a mountain-shaped pile. Press the back of a spoon into the top to make a well for the gravy. Place the sausages around the base and pour the gravy over the top, so that it runs down the side, like lava, before bringing to the table. Or pour over the gravy at the table for maximum dramatic effect!

JACKET POTATOES WITH CHILLI

I appreciate that there are a lot of potatoes in this section of the book, but there's nothing more comforting and traditional at this time of year than a spud! Get a big batch of chilli on the go and loads of toppings in little bowls and you'll keep your guests cosy all night. Of course, if you don't want to make the chilli, you can't go too wrong with baked beans and cheese...

PREP: 30 minutes
COOKING: 1–1½ hours

SERVES 4

4 large baking potatoes or 8 mini baking potatoes, washed and thoroughly dried

for the chilli
1 tbsp light olive oil
1 onion, diced
2 garlic cloves, finely chopped
1 red or orange pepper, chopped into 1cm chunks
400g lean minced beef or veggie substitute
2 tbsp mild chilli powder
2 tsp cocoa powder
½ tsp ground cumin
1 tsp chipotle chilli paste (optional)
1 x 400g tin of kidney beans, drained and rinsed
1 x 400g tin of black beans, drained and rinsed
1 x 400g tin of chopped tomatoes
300g passata
salt and black pepper

for the topping
100g Red Leicester cheese, grated
4 spring onions, thinly sliced
1 x 300g tub of sour cream
30g fresh coriander, leaves only

optional extra toppings
chopped chives, crumbled bacon, guacamole

Preheat the oven to 200°C/180°C fan/gas 6.

Heat the olive oil in a heavy-based pan over a medium–high heat. Add the onion and cook for a few minutes until beginning to soften, then add the garlic and pepper and cook for another 8–10 minutes, stirring often, until the pepper and onion are soft.

Prick each potato several times with a fork and pop into the oven on the middle shelf to bake for 1–1½ hours for large potatoes, less for smaller ones, until cooked all the way through. You can test them by piercing the skin with a knife or skewer – it should glide in easily.

Meanwhile, add the mince to the softened onion and pepper and season with salt and pepper. Break the mince up with a spoon and let it brown in the pan with the vegetables, then add the chilli powder, cocoa powder, cumin and chipotle paste, if using, and stir through to coat the meat and vegetables in the spices.

Tip all the drained beans into the pan and stir to mix. Add the tinned tomatoes and passata, reduce the heat to low, cover and cook for 30 minutes, stirring occasionally, then take the lid off and cook for another 30 minutes to reduce and thicken, stirring occasionally to prevent it from sticking.

To serve, place your topping ingredients into separate small bowls (plus any optional extras) and bring them to the table. Serve the potatoes topped with chilli and let everyone pile on their own toppings.

PUMPKIN SPICE CUPCAKES

I make a jar of pumpkin spice and use it throughout autumn and winter, stirred into porridge and hot chocolate and in all kinds of baking. You can buy pumpkin purée online and in some supermarkets or follow my recipe here. Decorate your cupcakes with sweets or edible glitter or make these cute marzipan pumpkins.

PREP: 25 minutes (not including making purée)
COOKING: 25 minutes
COOLING AND DECORATING: 40 minutes
MAKES 12

for the pumpkin spice mix
8 tbsp ground cinnamon
2 tbsp ground nutmeg
1 1/2 tbsp ground ginger
1 tbsp ground allspice
3 tsp ground cloves

for the cupcakes
1 tbsp pumpkin spice mix
1/2 tbsp baking powder
a pinch of salt
1/2 tsp bicarbonate of soda
140g plain flour
55g butter, softened
100g caster sugar
2 1/2 tbsp soft brown sugar
1 large egg
90ml milk
125g pumpkin purée

for the frosting
125g cream cheese
50g butter, softened
125g icing sugar
1 tsp vanilla extract
2 tsp ground cinnamon

essential equipment:
muffin tin and cupcake cases
stand mixer or electric beaters
piping bag fitted with a large
  nozzle
blender

Preheat the oven to 190°C/170°C fan/gas 5. Line a muffin tin with 12 paper or foil cupcake cases. For the spice mix, measure the ingredients out into a small jar and shake well to combine. Screw the lid on the jar and keep in a dry place for future use.

Add the dry cupcake ingredients to a mixing bowl and stir together with a spoon. In the bowl of a stand mixer, or in a mixing bowl using electric beaters, cream the butter and both sugars together until light and fluffy. Add in the egg and mix well to fully incorporate. Using a spoon,
stir in the milk and pumpkin purée.

Add the dry ingredients to the wet, stirring until they're only just incorporated but not over-mixed. Scoop the batter into the cupcake cases and bake for about 25 minutes, or until they are golden brown and a toothpick inserted into the centre of each cake comes out clean. Leave to cool in the tin for a few minutes, before turning out and cooling on a wire rack.

Make the frosting by adding the cream cheese and butter to the bowl of a stand mixer and beating until smooth (or use electric beaters). Add the icing sugar, one spoonful at a time, until it is all incorporated and the icing is smooth. Beat in the vanilla and cinnamon and whip for a few minutes on a higher speed until thick and fluffy. Spoon the icing into a large piping bag fitted with a nozzle of your choice (I used a plain one).

Once the cupcakes have cooled completely, pipe the icing in a swirl onto the top of each cake. You can decorate your iced cupcakes any way you'd like, adding black and orange sprinkles, Halloween sweets, leaf shapes cut from ready-made fondant icing or little marzipan pumpkins.

Pumpkin purée
Cut 1 small pumpkin (big ones for Halloween are likely to be too watery) in half and remove the seeds and stringy bits with a spoon. Cover the cut sides in tin foil and bake in an oven preheated to 170°C/150°C fan/gas 3½ for 1 hour, or until the flesh is very tender. Scoop the flesh away from the skin and purée in a blender.

Mini marzipan pumpkins
Knead 100g marzipan on a clean surface until warmed up and more pliable. Drip several drops of orange food colouring onto the marzipan and knead the colour through until the whole lump of marzipan is an even orange colour. Roll into 12 little balls, then flatten them slightly and use the back of a knife to make indentations like the ridges on the rind of a pumpkin. Create little stalks by rolling a little marzipan between your fingers and pop these on top before placing your finished pumpkins on top of your frosting!

CHAI LATTES

I can't wait for autumn, when I obsess over everything chai and pumpkin spice flavoured. We had these delicious warming drinks at our bonfire party, huddled round the fire pit as it got dark and just before we toasted marshmallows – it was bliss!

PREP: 5 minutes
COOKING: 25 minutes

SERVES 4-5

600ml milk of your choice (whole cow's milk, coconut milk or non-dairy alternatives)
a pinch of ground cinnamon
1 tsp brown sugar
cinnamon sticks, to serve (optional)

for the spiced tea
700ml water
1 thumb-sized piece of fresh ginger, peeled and roughly chopped
2 cloves
1 tsp ground cinnamon
½ tsp ground cardamom or 4 cardamom pods
½ tsp ground nutmeg
1 tsp whole black peppercorns
2 tbsp loose leaf black tea
2 tbsp brown sugar

Essential equipment:
milk frothing wand or hand-held blender

Pour the water for the spiced tea into a saucepan and add the ginger, cloves, cinnamon, cardamom, nutmeg and peppercorns. Bring to a simmer over a medium heat. Allow to simmer for 5-8 minutes, to infuse.

Remove the pan from the heat and add the tea. Cover the pan and allow the tea to steep for 10 minutes. Add the sugar and stir gently to dissolve. Strain the sweetened, spiced tea through a sieve to remove the whole spices and tea leaves. You can now chill the tea to use later or keep it warm while you prepare the milk.

Warm the milk in a saucepan with the cinnamon and sugar until it reaches simmering point, with little bubbles forming around the outside of the pan; don't let it boil. If you have a milk frothing wand, you can use it here, but if not, you can use a hand-held blender to create a nice foam.

If you've chilled the tea, warm it gently in a saucepan over a medium-low heat.

Pour 120ml of your spiced tea into each cup, then top with the warm, frothed milk and serve with a stick of cinnamon, if you like.

FRIENDS' NIGHT IN

A friends' night in might not be an occasion you put any effort into on the regular. Maybe you've had a long week and just want to crack open a wine, with the TV on in the background and have a good old natter. Sometimes though, especially if your friends don't live so locally, it's nice to make a bit more of a plan and put a little more effort into what you do when you see each other.

We often have friends to stay as we don't live particularly close to a lot of them, which means we see them a bit less but have much more quality time spent together when we do meet up. These are some of my favourite evenings and have made for some of my favourite memories.

For a great friends' night in, it's worth considering some garish pyjamas or a fluffy onesie, a movie or selection of movies you've either never seen before or love to pieces, games, a heap of snacks and drinks (see snack bingo on pages 180–181) and some face masks, eye masks or other nice pamper treats. I also like to make it a bit more cosy by bringing out the throws or grabbing a duvet from upstairs.

You could always consider doing something a bit more fun like building an inside den (see page 218) or keep it a bit more low-key and simply sip on hot chocolate and cheers to the week ahead with some trash TV and a pair of cosy socks.

SNACK BINGO

PRETZELS	POPCORN	NACHOS	GUACAMOLE
COOKIE DOUGH	STRAWBERRIES	CRUDITÉS	FLAVOURED RICE CAKES
CHIPS	GUMMY SWEETS	CHOCOLATE RAISINS	CRISPS
ICE CREAM	POTATO WEDGES	COOKIES	MINI DOUGHNUTS
BREADSTICKS	CHOCOLATE BARS	HUMMUS	STRAWBERRY LACES

Mix up your snacks whenever you have people over, I find the weirder the combo the better and a good balance of sweet and savoury – here are my favourite snack ideas to work your way through!

DOUGH BALLS	FROZEN GRAPES	FLAPJACKS	NUTS AND SEEDS
ROCKY ROAD	MINI MARSHMALLOWS	RASPBERRIES	CHOCOLATE BUTTONS
FLYING SAUCERS	FROZEN YOGHURT	BANANA CHIPS	CHICKEN GOUJONS
APPLE SLICES AND PEANUT BUTTER	GARLIC BREAD	BROWNIES	BLUEBERRIES
CHEESE STRAWS	MALTESERS	CUPCAKES	MINI PIZZA BITES

STAYING GUESTS

This truly encapsulates the main reason for me wanting to write this book, as I wholeheartedly believe it's not just the effort you make with food, drink and entertaining that enables you to be a hostess. A huge part of it is just making people feel comfortable and at home when they are staying with you and sometimes it's the smallest and easiest gestures that can do that! Having been a very nervous house guest when growing up, I know all too well that those little things that someone can do to make you feel at ease can go a really long way.

Whenever I have a guest to stay, I think it's nice to think about the things they love to eat, snacks they might want and any beverages they might love, especially people who visit quite regularly. My mum's favourite tea is a very specific one from M&S, so I always make sure I have a box of that in my cupboard to save her bringing her own tea bags – you don't want people to feel like they need to bring their own home comforts to your house or you may as well delete your hostess title!

If you have guests staying over, I also think it's nice to ask what they might want for breakfast. My friend Tanya loves Greek yoghurt, berries and honey (and occasionally we'll really push the boat out and do pancakes, see page 20) so I know she'll be happy if we have that when she's here. As well as asking if they have a breakfast preference, it's good to check people's dietary requirements too. If you're planning a huge sleepover or have friends staying for the first time, you could be unaware of an allergy or intolerance to specific foods, so it's better to ask than to whip something up that they can't eat, when you might not have an alternative.

One of the main things I like to do when I have a guest staying is make the bedroom feel cosy and 'theirs'. What I mean by that is giving them everything they could possibly need and enabling them to feel as though the minute they step into that room, or onto that airbed, they feel as though it's their space. Fresh sheets are a good start here, as getting into a bed that someone else has already slept in immediately says 'this isn't mine'. You know that amazing feeling when you peel back crisp hotel bed sheets? I love my guests to feel that way when staying with me – even if we don't all have 1,000 thread count sheets and giant steamers to recreate this exactly, a little bit of fabric softener and a throw are a great touch. I try and clear the spare bedroom of anything that is personal to me or to my partner (the odd charity shop bag, camera equipment or empty suitcase) because, again, you want this bedroom to feel like a place they can fully relax and make use of the space with their own things.

One of the first things I like to check when I get into a hotel room is the mini bar and the little miniatures in the bathroom, and for that very reason I like to leave a tray of useful things in the guest room which include snacks, headphones, a spare phone charger, sleep mist, spare toothbrush, eye mask, lip balm, dry shampoo, hand sanitiser, hand cream, face mask, chewing gum and a fresh towel and flannel. If this all feels a bit much for you and your guest is only sleeping on a blow-up mattress on the floor next to you, you can still leave something like a little chocolate on the pillow with a fresh towel as a nice touch!

Depending on the time of year, I also like to create a bit of ambience by lighting candles, popping some fresh flowers in a vase and placing these on the bedside table or mantelpiece, or by adding a nice green house plant! If you have a guest staying who has recently celebrated something - a job promotion, passing an exam or reaching a personal milestone - or you just

want to tell someone how much they mean to you, it might be nice to leave a message on a chalkboard, peg board or to write a card to pop beside the bed for them to read. Failing that, you could just write up a little welcome message, or it's also very useful to pop the WiFi code on there so they aren't having to ask you every half an hour for each of their devices. Another thing I feel adds a really nice personal touch is to display photographs of you and your friends or old memories you may have shared together. If, like me, you have loads of frames around the house with different friends in each, you can move these around and put one in the spare bedroom while that guest is staying, as something to look back on and reminisce over!

BEING A GOOD GUEST

As much as it's down to the hostess to make you feel comfortable, I also think there are a few things to think about if you are a guest and you've been invited somewhere:

Ask if the host needs any help. You've had your invite and you've got the date in your diary but make sure you reach out to the host and ask if there is anything you can do to help, or anything you can bring along to make their life a little easier before the party or event!

Bringing a gift? Don't go too overboard, and try and think a little outside the box. If you have the time, bringing something homemade is a lovely sentiment. My mum brought marmalade that she'd made herself last time she visited, as well as a posy of sweet peas picked from her garden. At our house-warming party, we received lots of beautiful flowers, vases, terrariums, bottles of alcohol and neon signs, but one gift that stood out to me a lot was from a friend who

had brought her two favourite recipe books for me to add to my small but growing collection and it was just perfect!

Don't be too early, don't stay too late! You're given a time to arrive for a reason and if you decide to show up too early, the host is most likely running around with half their outfit on, wet hair, a wooden spoon in one hand and a balloon to blow up in the other. You being there will only add another layer of stress as they will feel they need to grab you a drink and get the canapés out early! In addition to arriving early, being the party straggler is also not something you want to be labelled. We all love a good time and never want a party to be over, but don't be that person who stays hours after even the host has gone to bed (at least not without offering to help clear up the mess).

Saying thank you! I'm a woman who loves manners and I think it's important when someone has hosted you or a party (particularly a large one that you know has involved many a breakdown and a pretty penny) that it's only right to thank them. This doesn't need to be a huge, expensive thank you – just a card, email or text is enough. I have to say I'm not always the best at writing out a thank-you card and usually opt for a text message or a bunch of flowers. However, being on the receiving end of a little thank-you card landing on your doormat is actually very lovely, and I always appreciate the sentiment behind it.

Mum's tip

Keep a book/journal of any dinner parties you have had with a list of who attended, their intolerances or preferences and the food you served. When inviting the same people back you don't want to cook them something they can't eat or the same thing they all ate last time without realising (unless of course they requested it because it was a huge success).

CEREAL PARTY

Now, before you rip me to Shreddies for having a section on cereal (see what I did there?!), I wanted to include this section as it's something I do often and guests really enjoy. It's SO simple and incredibly easy but it is so much fun. I had my friends to stay last summer and as there were quite a lot of us, I poured as many different varieties of cereal that I could/had lying around into jars on the breakfast bar, put out the bowls and spoons and poured the milk into a jug for people to help themselves. Do you remember as a child, going to stay with someone who had the little multi-pack of cereal and it being the best thing to wake up to and make that very conscious and difficult decision of 'which one?'. I often had to fight my brother for the Coco Pops! It can be healthy or chocolatey, it can cater to all with varieties of milk and it can be a bit of a childhood throwback. I'm also a huge lover of cereal and having all my favourite varieties in jars on my kitchen shelves is visually and practically very pleasing. I've listed a few examples of things you can have if you're planning on having lots of people to stay over and want to throw a bit of a cereal party to start the day off in the right way!

YOUR CEREAL BASE
Granola, muesli, porridge, Cheerios, Weetabix, bran flakes, corn flakes, Coco Pops – the choice is yours! (If you choose muesli, you can upgrade to a Bircher muesli by soaking your oats overnight in a little apple juice.)

MILK, DAIRY-FREE ALTERNATIVES & JUICE
Juices make a delicious alternative to milk when you're having porridge, muesli or oat-based cereals. They add sweetness, so be careful not to overdo it if your granola is already sweetened. If you need a chocolate hit first thing in the morning, you could stir a tablespoon of cocoa powder into your milk before pouring it over your cereal:
almond milk, oat milk, soya milk, coconut drink, hemp milk, goat's milk or regular cow's milk, apple juice, mango juice, orange juice, pineapple juice, or any mixed juice

FRESH FRUIT
Slice them up and pile them high:
strawberries, blueberries, mango, bananas, grapes, plums, apples, raspberries, pineapple, pears, oranges, melon, pomegranate seeds

YOGHURT & DAIRY-FREE ALTERNATIVES
A chance to add some tang and creaminess to your bowl!
coconut yoghurt, Greek-style yoghurt, soya yoghurt, honey yoghurt, fruit yoghurt

DRIED FRUIT, NUTS & SEEDS
You can add richness and crunch with dried fruit, nuts and seeds, raisins, sultanas, apricots, cranberries, mango slices, figs, dates, cherries, hazelnuts, walnuts, pecans, cashews, macadamia nuts, almonds, chia seeds, sunflower seeds, pumpkin seeds, coconut flakes, cacao nibs

SOMETHING TO DRIZZLE
Top it all off with a little trickle of something sweet:
honey, maple syrup, agave nectar, date nectar

SOMETHING SWEET
Now for the fun bit...
chocolate chips, yoghurt-coated raisins, mini marshmallows, sprinkles

Win

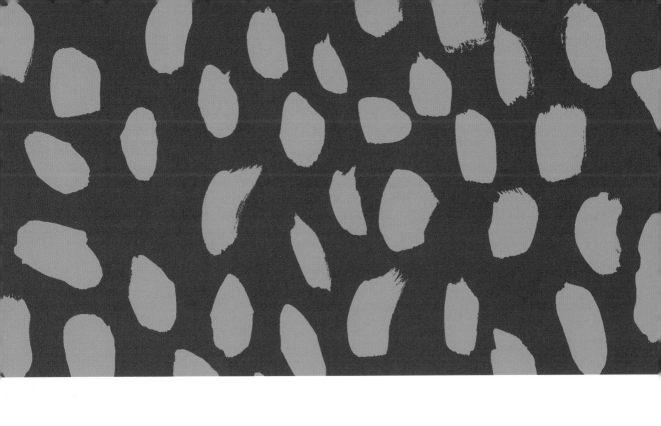

ter

The countdown has finally begun and the crisp winter cold has crept upon us. Frosty and fog-filled mornings lie ahead as we all start to prep for one of the busiest times of the year in terms of being an all-round hostess. 'Tis the season to be jolly and I am very jolly towards the start of winter as I prepare for what is essentially the most excitement-fuelled time of the year!

I can appreciate that not everybody reading this will celebrate Christmas, but it is a huge part of my year and when it comes to all things Christmas and festive, I am an A+ student (even if I say so myself). I love absolutely everything about this holiday season: the abundance of coloured fairy lights glowing from inside people's houses and draped over everything in mine (if I can help it), putting cinnamon on and in everything, lighting all the festive spice candles, getting crafty, wrapping presents and having the perfect excuse to throw mini parties for everyone. Even if you don't actually celebrate Christmas yourself, it's the perfect way to end the year! You can do a Christmas work party, a Christmas friends' party, a Christmas movie night, A 'Let's Exchange Gifts' sleepover – the amount of socialising through December is pretty much endless (if you hate socialising, December will not be the month for you, and I'd advise you hibernate now).

> It's the time of year when I'll spend more time in my loungewear and PJs, eating leftover Christmas food, hiding under blankets and doing puzzles.

I love that it's the time of year when everyone is in such a great mood, spirits are high and there's a buzz in the air with all the anticipation for Christmas Day. Even with all the last-minute present dashing in town on Christmas Eve, people still manage to crack a smile to one another (although this is more than likely a very knowing smile of 'we both left this too late didn't we mate?').

After the plans and parties during Christmas and the post-Christmas come-down on Boxing Day, and those weird days after, where time doesn't really exist, it's New Year's Eve! We often go away with family for New Year, but it's

also the perfect opportunity to throw a party to bring in the new year on a high. (See pages 222-223 for some of my top New Year hosting tips.)

It's then that we start a fresh year, setting goals (or not in some cases) for the months to come. I always find January to be a very slow month, so I think it's important to arrange some time with friends. Maybe organise to have a little getaway together or even just make tent dens with snacks and your favourite movies in your living room, on those rainy grey days where you couldn't possibly face leaving the house (see page 218).

Other things through winter that bring me hosting joy include Valentine's Day (or Galentine's/Palentine's, depending on how you like to spend this occasion). It's the perfect time to make a bit of effort for the people you love and appreciate, whether that's your BFF or your other half.

On very rare occasions, winter also brings us the possibility of snow (or usually the case for those of us living in the south of England, a bit of slush). Waking up to the clean, white and fresh blanket that covers everything is like waking up in a magical winter wonderland. On days like these it's important to wear at least five layers and run around like a child throwing snowballs and making snowmen (mostly because it will probably last one day maximum, and you need to make the absolute most of it). I love whipping on my scarf, hat, gloves and Wellington boots, going for a walk and hearing and feeling the snow crunch beneath my feet while watching the robins bobbing about. Nala loves the snow too, and it's the perfect excuse to dress her up!

As much as I love being outside on days like these, the reality is that most winter days are quite grey and rainy, so it's a season of indoor crafts and activities. It's the time of the year where I'll spend more time in my loungewear and PJs, eating leftover Christmas food, hiding under blankets and doing puzzles!

WINTER TO-DO LIST

○ Update your bedding for a more festive theme.

○ Plan a Christmas or New Year's Eve party (see pages 222-223).

○ Go ice skating - find the nearest pop-up outdoor rink to where you live.

○ Visit a Christmas market.

○ Buy the tackiest Christmas jumper you can find and wear it for the majority of December.

○ Make and decorate a gingerbread house (see page 208).

○ Pick your tree and decorate it.

○ Build a snowman and have a snowball fight (if you're lucky enough to get snow).

○ Watch your favourite Christmas movies.

○ Plan a secret Santa gift giving.

○ Send your Christmas cards.

○ Cover your house with fairy lights (inside and out).

○ Make a Christmas playlist.

○ Put a wreath on your front door.

○ Decorate your home or shelves with some fresh green foliage.

○ Dry orange slices for decorations (see page 202).

○ Sing carols.

○ Eat mince pies.

○ Look at all the lights on neighbouring houses.

○ Reflect on your year and make new goals and plans for the next one.

○ Arrange a nice day for your other half or friends, for Valentine's/ Palentine's.

○ Make a den in your living room with snacks and movies (see page 218).

○ Start a scrapbook with photos from the year.

○ Have a board games day.

CHRISTMAS

Christmas, the season of goodwill, high spirits, hosting and heaps of fairy lights and food. It's a great time of year to celebrate, as it lends itself to months of potential in terms of planning, prep and endless creativity. I like to start celebrating Christmas as early as possible because everything leading up to the big day is just as exciting for me! It's that feeling of warmth and giddiness from those around you, the decorations and the togetherness that Christmas brings.

It's also the best time for your inner hostess, because the baking goes into overdrive and the number of visitors, and amount of visiting you're doing, triples. I like to be really organised at this time of year and plan my days quite far in advance. One of the first things you need to decide is where you're going to be on Christmas Day. Are you hosting (good luck!) or are you going to someone else's home instead? If it's the latter, make sure you offer any help you can. Maybe you can make the dessert, bring a lovely side dish that can accompany the turkey (see my recipe for posh cauliflower cheese on page 215) or be in charge of games or Christmas Eve activities. Wherever you are going, you should be sure that you are responsible for at least one element in order to fulfil your inner hostess and to take a little pressure off the Christmas Day chef!

If you are doing a Christmas party yourself, or deciding to bite the bullet and host people at your house for Christmas Day, here are a few things you need to consider:

Mum's tip

If you have families coming over for dinner, it's quite nice to create a smaller, lower table for the little ones to sit together and eat their meals at. It feels like their personal dining experience and adult chat doesn't need to be so censored.

NUMBER OF GUESTS

Get this nailed early on. If someone is likely to ask for a plus-one, be prepared for that too; once you know the number of guests you will be having, you can start planning everything else around that.

TABLE AND DINNERWARE

You need to be sure you have the right amount of space for your guests and the right numbers of plates, glasses, cutlery, serving dishes etc. Our family has been known to extend tables with huge sheets of plywood and have other family members bring extra chairs along! I think this all adds to the homemade element. It's also good to think about how you will decorate the table. Will you need to buy a new tablecloth and napkins? Maybe make some name places and add a touch of creativity in some areas! (See page 207 for my cute mini wreath place names.)

FOOD AND DRINK

VERY important! Christmas is of course the time for sharing, caring and spending as much quality time with the people you love, but it's also the time for cramming in as much food and drink as we possibly can – there is a reason those tacky oversized Christmas jumpers come in so handy! Plan your food in advance. Ask your guests their dietary requirements and keep a note of them – your auntie may have been a vegetarian last year, but it's worth checking in again in case this has changed. Create a list of all the things you will need to buy for each meal and take into consideration that the amount you will need of each item will double if you have lots of guests (we've all been there when we thought one bag of peas would feed more than twelve people...).

I think it's a really nice touch to ask guests what their favourite dish in a Christmas dinner is, so that you can be sure it is being served. I once had a Christmas dinner that had no mashed potato to accompany it (and I know full well this is not a traditional part of a Christmas dinner but I just love mashed potato) and it just didn't seem right! It's so lovely to be able to offer each person their one dream side dish. It could end up meaning you're cooking a little more than normal, but

Mum's tip

Success of a seated dinner party (apart from the food) rides on who you place next to each other. Before your guests arrive decide who is sitting where to eliminate confusion when the time comes to sit down.

if you are prepared to ask certain people to help you out, it shouldn't make too much of a difference, and you're guaranteed to have no disappointed, hungry people at your table. It's not just the Christmas dinner food you need to be thinking about, it's the Christmas Eve snacks, the Christmas morning breakfast, the appetisers, the dessert, the cheeseboard, the soft drinks and the alcoholic drinks! Hosting Christmas can very easily become quite expensive. This is why being as prepared as possible in this area and allocating your guests something they are in charge of is important! For our Christmas day, we had someone else in charge of dessert, and someone else in charge of the cheeseboard, and that was a real weight lifted off my shoulders! One other very important point to consider is to ORDER YOUR TURKEY EARLY!

ENTERTAINMENT

I like to buy novelty Christmas hats and place them on individual chairs at the table, or maybe some funny face masks or scratch cards! You've always got the terrible jokes inside the crackers to create a bit of a laugh too! Besides the fact that the TV will host an endless stream of great movies and shows all day, it's nice to have other things you can do with your guests that create fun memories, and there are board games and games consoles that offer endless fun. More traditional ideas include things like charades, 'I went to the market and I bought...', 'Would you rather', 'Who am I?', or the Post-It note game, all without leaving the table! We also love games like Bananagrams, Dobble, Scrabble and Rummikub to play at the table after dinner. (See my game guide on pages 216–217.)

STAYING GUESTS

If you have guests who are going to be staying, you need to consider fresh towels, fresh bedding, clearing the spare room and providing breakfast the next morning. If you have guests needing a taxi home, it's

> **Must-see Christmas movies:**
>
> *The Holiday*
> *Elf*
> *Love Actually*
> *Arthur Christmas*
> *Home Alone (either 1 or 2)*
> *Jingle All The Way*
> *It's a Wonderful Life*
> *The Muppet Christmas Carol*
> *The Santa Clause*
> *How the Grinch Stole Christmas*
> *Miracle on 34th Street*
> *The Snowman*
> *Polar Express*

also worth thinking about booking this in advance too, as Christmas can get very busy!

Whether you are hosting, dual-hosting or visiting someone else at Christmas-time, there are definitely elements of the list above that will help you.

Christmas really is the most magical time of the year, and although the days feel shorter and the weather has taken a turn, everyone coming together to celebrate, decorate and make memories makes for the best month of the year. Whether you celebrate Christmas or not, there is so much to get involved in!

There are always so many things to try and cram in before the big day, so I thought I'd write a little tick list so you know exactly where you are and what you still need to do before the whirlwind is over for another year.

Mum's tip

If you're doing a dinner party, always preheat your serving ware and plates in advance. If you don't have space in the oven, give them a quick run through the dishwasher and they will come out sparkling and warm! If you don't have a dishwasher, hot water in the sink is also good for this.

CHRISTMAS TO-DO LIST

○ Ask your Christmas Day host if you can be in charge of anything.

○ Donate to a homeless shelter, give a gift, or shoe box of gifts via the charity Link to Hope, to families and children who will not receive a present, or take nice food to a food bank.

○ Take a Christmas family photo.

○ Do a Christmas puzzle.

○ Buy Christmas crackers.

○ Burn your favourite festive candles.

○ Buy a new tree ornament/bauble.

○ Find a party outfit that sparkles.

○ Watch a different Christmas movie every weekend in the lead-up to Christmas (or if you're like me, every night).

○ Dance like nobody is watching to a Christmas playlist.

○ Eat a candy cane.

○ Wear a red lipstick.

○ Visit a Christmas carol service in your local church, a play/ nativity or a carol concert.

○ Buy a Christmas chocolate tin (Roses are my favourite).

○ Kiss someone under the mistletoe.

AROMATIC ORANGE SLICES

LOW EFFORT

When it comes to homemade decoration for Christmas time, you can't get anything easier to make than simple dried orange slices. I love their natural, rustic look and, what's more, as they dry out in the oven they fill your house with a wonderful citrus smell. You can either scatter them across your mantelpiece or table, or string them together to make a garland.

You will need:

oranges
sharp knife
chopping board
pencil (optional)
baking sheets
baking parchment
thin ribbon or twine (optional)

How to:

1 Turn on your oven and set the temperature to the lowest possible setting. Slice each orange carefully into thin, 1cm-wide rounds, cutting widthways around the 'waist' of the orange. Discard the end pieces.

2 If you want to make a garland from the dried slices, use a pencil to open out the centre of the orange to make the hole that you can later use to thread the ribbon through.

3 Line baking sheets with baking parchment to stop the orange slices sticking as they dry out. Lay all the orange slices on to the lined baking sheets in a single layer, making sure that they are not overlapping.

4 Pop the baking sheets into the oven and leave them in there to dry out – this will take about 4 hours. Turn the orange slices over regularly to make sure that they dry out evenly and don't stick. If the slices start to brown or burn, open the oven door and leave it slightly ajar.

5 When the orange peel has hardened and the flesh has dried out, remove the orange slices from the oven and leave them to cool on the baking sheets. (They might feel a little tacky when straight out of the oven, but they will dry out further as they cool.)

6 If you are hanging the orange slices from your Christmas tree or using them to make a garland, once they are completely cool, thread a length of ribbon or twine through the central hole. Tie the ends together to make a loop.

TIP

If you want to dry whole limes or other small citrus fruits, cut slits from top to bottom around each fruit, leaving about 1cm of uncut peel at each end. Dry in a low oven for 6–8 hours.

CHRISTMAS PLACE NAMES

Setting the table for Christmas lunch is something I look forward to most during the festive season. Little details such as personalised place names really make it feel like a special event.

For each place name, you will need:

1.5m mini holly leaf garland with mini holly berries
10cm diameter polyester donut ring
mini coloured bells and thin florist's wire (optional)
parcel tags
white pen
ribbon or string

How to:

1 Unravel the mini holly garland. Take the polyester donut ring and, starting at one end of the garland, wrap the mini holly garland around the ring, passing it through the central hole each time you wrap it round. Take care to space each wrap evenly around the ring so there are no visible gaps and the two ends meet. Twist the two ends of the mini holly garland together to secure.

2 If you want to add little bells, take a short piece of florist's wire and thread on a mini coloured bell. Twist the ends of the wire together to make one 'pin' and wrap it around the donut ring. Repeat with more bells, placing them randomly around the ring.

3 Write your guest's names onto the parcel tags and tie onto the festive rings with ribbon or string.

Mum's tip

If you're going to someone's house for a party, try not to get there early! The host will have planned for your arrival and timed things accordingly, so a very early entrance could derail their plans.

GINGERBREAD HOUSE

I love how magical these look – if you cut out the windows and door you can even put a little battery-operated tea light inside so it glows at night. I've gone for quite a Scandi theme with my house, but you can also go completely the opposite way and cover your house in all different coloured sweets.

PREP: 30 minutes plus chilling to make and shape the biscuits, plus decorating time
COOKING: 12–18 minutes

SERVES 6–8

115g unsalted butter, softened
90g light muscovado sugar
60ml dark treacle
1 tbsp ground ginger
$\frac{1}{2}$ tbsp ground cinnamon
1 tsp ground cloves
1 tsp bicarbonate of soda
220g plain flour
1–2 tbsp water

for the icing
1 egg white
225g icing sugar

to decorate
silver balls
gummy sweets
lollipops

essential equipment:
piping bag fitted with a small plain nozzle

In the bowl of a stand mixer or in a large bowl using a wooden spoon, cream together the butter, sugar, treacle, spices and bicarbonate of soda. Beat until smooth and creamy, then fold through the flour and enough water to make a stiff dough. Wrap the dough in cling film and chill for 30 minutes to firm up. Preheat the oven to 190°C/170°C fan/gas 5.

Cut two large pieces of non-stick baking paper and divide the dough in half. Using a rolling pin, roll out half the dough between the two pieces, to a thickness of about 7mm. Peel back the top layer of the paper and, using a sharp knife, cut out 2 rectangles for the side walls, each 7 x 13cm. Remove the excess dough around the cut out rectangles, leaving the shapes on the baking paper. Slide the shapes straight onto a baking sheet, still on the baking paper. Carefully cut one window in each, no bigger than a few centimetres square so that you don't risk weakening the wall.

Roll out the other half of dough between two pieces of non-stick baking paper in the same way, and cut out 2 slightly bigger rectangles for the roof, each 7 x 15cm, again removing the excess dough from around the shapes and sliding the shapes onto a baking sheet, on the baking paper. Repeat with the remaining dough trimmings to make the end walls of your house by cutting two arrow shapes, 7cm square and with a point measuring out to 15cm at the apex. You can cut a rectangular door in one end, if you like. Re-roll any leftover dough and cut out trees, animals or stars to add to your scene.

Bake the gingerbread pieces for 12–18 minutes, or until slightly darker around the edges and firm. If the shapes have sagged a little in baking, you can trim then straighten the lines while they are still warm and before they harden. Leave undisturbed on the baking sheets to cool completely.

Make the icing by whisking the egg white and icing sugar together in a bowl until thick. You need it to be quite thick so that it can stick your house together. Put the icing into a piping bag fitted with a small, plain nozzle.

When the gingerbread is completely cool, use the icing as glue to stick the side walls to the front and back walls. (You might need some help to hold the pieces steady as you build.) Let the joints set before adding the roof. Pipe the icing along all the edges and carefully stick the roof on, with a ridge of icing along the top. The rest of the decorating is up to you! You can pipe icing decorations, or use the icing like glue to add silver balls and sweets.

CANDY CANE CUPCAKES

As you probably know, I like to go all out at Christmas and these little candy cane cupcakes are perfect to have in the middle of the table when you have people round as they look so pretty. They are like edible decorations! See pages 212-213 for photograph.

See pages 212-213 for photograph.

PREP: 25 minutes
COOKING: 15-20 minutes
COOLING: at least 40 minutes

MAKES 12

60g unsalted butter, softened
150g caster sugar
1 large egg
1 tsp vanilla extract
90g plain flour
50g cocoa powder
1/2 tsp bicarbonate of soda
a pinch of salt
50ml buttermilk
50ml water
24 mini candy canes, to decorate

for the peppermint buttercream
250g unsalted butter, softened
2 tsp vanilla extract
1 tsp peppermint extract (optional)
300g icing sugar
3 tsp whole milk, if needed
5 candy canes

essential equipment:
muffin tin and cupcake cases
stand mixer or electric beaters
piping bag fitted with a large nozzle

Preheat the oven to 190°C/170°C fan/gas 5 and line a muffin tin with 12 Christmassy papers or foil cupcake cases.

In the bowl of a stand mixer or using electric beaters, cream together the butter and sugar until light and fluffy. Add the egg, then beat the mixture well to be sure it is fully incorporated. Add the vanilla.

In a separate bowl, combine the flour, cocoa powder, bicarb and salt. In a jug, combine the buttermilk and water.

Add one third of your dry ingredients to the creamed butter mixture and mix well to combine, then add half the buttermilk and water. Beat well. Add another third of the dry ingredients, beat well, then the remaining wet ingredients, beating well again before adding the final third of the dry ingredients.

Spoon the batter into your lined muffin tin, so that the cups are two-thirds full. Bake for 15-20 minutes, or until a toothpick inserted in the centre of a cake comes out clean. Remove from the oven and allow the cakes to cool for a few minutes before turning out and cooling completely on a wire rack.

Make the buttercream by beating the butter, vanilla and peppermint extract, if using, until smooth and creamy, then add the icing sugar 1 tablespoon at a time. Whip the mixture on a higher speed for a few minutes to make it voluminous and light, adding a little milk a teaspoon at a time to loosen if it seems too stiff.

Place the 5 candy canes in a freezer bag and smash into small bits using a rolling pin. Reserving some of the crushed candy cane to decorate your cupcakes, tip the rest of the pieces into the buttercream and whip again for a few minutes. This will make the buttercream slightly pink.

Spoon the buttercream into a piping bag fitted with a plain or fluted nozzle and pipe it on to the tops of the cooled cupcakes. Add a mini candy cane or two to finish and sprinkle the reserved crushed candy cane over the top.

CANDY CANE MACARONS

These elegant festive sweets also make a great gift – pack them into a little box with some tissue paper and they'll look like they've come straight from a Parisian patisserie! See pages 212–213 for photograph.

PREP AND DECORATING:
1 hour
COOKING: 10 minutes

MAKES 12

100g icing sugar
90g ground almonds
2 egg whites
a pinch of cream of tartar
40g caster sugar
red gel food colouring
    (optional)
4–5 candy canes (ideally
    ones with green and red
    stripes)

for the ganache filling
300g white chocolate,
    chopped very small
150ml double cream
20g unsalted butter
a tiny pinch of salt
1 tsp peppermint extract

essential equipment:
piping bag fitted with a plain
    nozzle
food processor
stand mixer or electric
    beaters

Line two baking trays with non-stick baking paper. Fit a large piping bag with a plain nozzle.

Pulse the icing sugar and ground almonds together in a food processor a few times to combine and make sure that there are no lumps.

Whisk the egg whites in the (spotlessly clean) bowl of your stand mixer until frothy (or use a bowl and electric beaters), then add the cream of tartar and whisk until soft peaks form. Add the caster sugar, a spoonful at a time, until all the sugar has been added and the glossy mixture holds soft peaks.

Sift your blitzed almond and icing sugar into the egg whites and fold with a spatula until it falls in silky ribbons when you pour it off the spatula.

If you'd like the macarons to have swirly tops, add stripes of red colouring up the sides of a piping bag before spooning the batter in. Pipe the mixture onto the lined trays into 24 rounds, each 4cm across, trying not to let a little peak form at the top of each, by finishing the piping at the side of each one instead. Tap the trays on the work surface to release any trapped air bubbles, then leave to stand for 30 minutes to dry slightly. Preheat the oven to 190°C/170°C fan/gas 5.

Just before putting the trays in the oven, reduce the temperature to 160°C/140°C fan/gas 3 and bake for 10 minutes. The macarons should puff up and develop a little frill around the bottom edge. Remove the trays from the oven and allow the macarons to cool completely on the trays. Once completely cool, peel them carefully away from the baking paper. They will keep for 3–4 days in an airtight container.

For the ganache, put the chopped white chocolate in a heatproof bowl. Pour the cream into a saucepan and place over a medium-high heat, removing it from the heat just as it comes to boiling point. Pour the hot cream over the chopped chocolate and let it sit for a minute to let the chocolate start melting, then stir with a spatula until smooth. Add the butter and stir until it is melted through. Add the salt and half the peppermint extract. Taste, and if you'd like it a little more minty, add the remaining peppermint extract.

Sandwich a spoonful or two of filling between two macaron biscuits, and repeat to use up all the biscuits. Put the candy canes into a plastic freezer bag and crush them with a rolling pin. Tip out onto a plate and roll the edges of each macaron through them, so that the pieces stick to the ganache. As a final flourish use your red colouring to paint a festive stripe. Set your macarons on a pretty Christmassy plate and serve.

EXTRA SPECIAL CAULIFLOWER CHEESE

This is my luxurious cauliflower cheese dish - it is so rich and creamy with a festive nutty topping. You don't have to save it just for December though as it goes really well with most roast dinners. You can actually prepare it the day before and then finish it off just before you need it by adding the topping and giving it a final blast in the oven.

PREP: 15 minutes
COOKING: 1 hour

SERVES 6-8 as a side dish

900ml whole milk
½ onion
2 bay leaves
1 large cauliflower
50g unsalted butter, plus an extra knob for frying
50g plain flour
100g Gruyère, grated
50ml double cream
½ tsp ground nutmeg
20g hazelnuts, chopped (or blitzed until coarse in a food processor)
25g fresh breadcrumbs
20g mature Cheddar, grated
salt and black pepper

Pour the milk into a saucepan and add the half onion and bay leaves. Bring to a simmer, but don't let it boil. Remove the pan from the heat and leave to infuse for 20 minutes before straining out the onion and bay.

Meanwhile, bring a large pan of water to the boil and cut the cauliflower into even-sized medium to large florets. You can include the core too, just cut it up into the same size chunks. Add the cauliflower and a generous pinch of salt to the boiling water and cook for 6-10 minutes, or until tender but still al dente. Drain into a colander, shake and set aside to dry out a little.

Melt the 50g butter in a medium pan over a medium heat and, when it begins to foam, stir in the flour. Cook for 2 minutes, stirring with a spoon. Slowly pour in the infused milk, stirring all the time until you have a smooth, creamy sauce. Reduce the heat to low and simmer, stirring often, for 15 minutes.

Preheat the oven to 200°C/180°C fan/gas 6.

Stir the grated Gruyère into the sauce with the cream and nutmeg and season with salt and pepper.

Melt the knob of butter in a frying pan over a medium-high heat and, when it begins to foam, tip the chopped hazelnuts and breadcrumbs into the pan. Fry until crispy, then remove from the heat.

Tip the cauliflower into an ovenproof dish, pour the cheese sauce over the top, then sprinkle the grated Cheddar evenly over. (You can actually make it to this point the day before.) Sprinkle the crispy breadcrumbs and hazelnuts over the top and bake in the oven for about 20 minutes, until the cheese is bubbly and the top is golden brown.

GAMES

————

Games play an important role at any party, hang-out or seasonal celebration, especially in our house! They are usually what breaks the ice between guests who may not know each other so well, or for those that find conversation a little harder. It's also a great way of bringing out the best (or sometimes worst) in people as their competitive edge comes out.

Depending on the type of game you choose to play, it's usually a whole lot of fun and a lot of the evening is centred around it (and the food of course). There are definitely games that sit very well within certain types of get-together, so I wanted to list some of my favourite ones for you to make life a little simpler when planning a particular shindig.

THE CASUAL FAMILY GET- TOGETHER:

————

2–8 people

Scrabble
Monopoly
Rummikub
Bananagrams
Dobble
Trionimos
Linkee
Cluedo
Trivial Pursuit
Lattice
Family Fortunes
A deck of cards for other card games!
Bingo

THE FRIENDS SLEEPOVER:

————

4–8 people

90s Dream Phone
Dobble
Most Likely To...
Psych (App Game)
Linkee
Mr & Mrs (great for couples sleepovers)
Operation
Scrawl
Articulate
Speak Out
Pictionary
Funemployed
Claw Ninja

Mum's tip

A great, easy party game is to put a pile of fabric scraps, bin liners etc. into the middle of the room and get all the guests to make themselves an outfit to be judged. Be warned — this can get seriously competitive!

Mum's tip

You're never too old for pass the parcel! It's brilliant fun no matter your budget and you could include a little gift in every layer, or just a forfeit. I did one for my son's 18th birthday and his friends loved it. It's also very easy to theme!

THE MORE LIVELY HOUSE PARTY:

6–15 people

Bean Boozled
Beer Pong/Prosecco Pong
Giant Jenga
Twister
Rounders
Never Have I Ever (drinking edition)
'Who Am I' Post-It note game
Cards Against Humanity
What do you meme?
Accentuate
Boom Boom Balloon
Speak Out
Charades in groups
The voting game
Ring of Fire

DINNER TABLE GAMES:

4+ people

'Who Am I' Post-It note game
Charades
Old Maid
Deck of cards
Try Not to Laugh
Quiz – (Have a Quiz Master, choose a
    theme and do as individuals, pairs or
    teams. Having a Halloween Party? Make
    the quiz spooky themed)
Two Truths One Lie
Memory Game ('I went to the market
    and I bought...') – Continue around the
    table listing everyone's items until
    someone messes up or forgets
Most Likely To...

RAINY DAY DEN

Winter weather means that making plans can become a little more tricky, as the last thing you and your friends want is to get caught up in a rainstorm. On those days where you have friends over for the day or if they're staying for the evening and you just don't know how to add an element of fun, I like to whip out the 'Indoor Rainy Day Den'. For me, those rainy days are incredibly cosy. You don't feel bad about not leaving the house, you can wrap up warm under blankets, put on a favourite movie and have a good pile of snacks to hand. Instead of just all sitting on the sofa, which is what you'll do on an average rainy day, the den makes it that little bit more epic. Who doesn't like to feel like a big kid again by creating a den?

You'll need to channel your inner Bear Grylls and think a bit outside the box when it comes to building the structure of the den. Is there something you can hang your sheets to? Maybe a step ladder at one end, or you could string up a washing line between two solid points in your room and drape your sheets over the top. (I used my camera tripods but anything equally tall will work really well.) You'll then want big sheets of fabric, which you can of course pick up online, in a fabric shop, or just use some bed sheets – use some big bulldog clips to ensure the sheets cover and connect well.

The inside is a bit more of a personal preference but I like to line the bottom with cushions (makes it very cosy), add a bed-spread to make the floor and then line the back with even more cushions. I also like to put as many fairy lights in there as I can, and you can wrap them around any poles or strings that you are using to hold up the den.

Then, finally, you'll want some throws or blankets, or just bring your duvet down from your bed. The goal is just to feel like you've created a cosy, atmospheric little space that you and your friends will stay in, watching movies and eating all the snacks. I do feel like half the fun is in creating the den too. There will be major fails, walls will cave in and you could all end up in a heap under cushions, throws and mountains of material, but that is all part of it! It's purely a chance for you to get a bit more creative, have fun and make a day of it, even when the weather isn't on your side. And check out my nacho recipe on page 220 for the ultimate den snack...

Tick list for the ultimate hot chocolate

- Milk frother
- Chocolate to grate on top
- Double cream
- Mini marshmallows
- A chocolate flake

CHILLI BEEF NACHOS

Cold winter days are all about lounging around at home in something cosy, watching movies or just hanging out. For days like these, a big plate of nachos is just what is called for. I love all the extras that go with nachos – guac, refried beans, sour cream and salsa – so make sure you have plenty to go around.

PREP: 10 minutes
COOKING: 45 minutes

SERVES 4–6 as a big snack

for the beef chilli
1 tbsp olive oil
1 onion, finely chopped
1 garlic clove, finely chopped
300g lean minced beef
2 tbsp tomato paste
2 tsp chilli powder (mild, medium or hot – it's your choice!)
50ml water
salt and black pepper

for the nachos
1 bag of salted tortilla chips (160–180g)
200g mild Cheddar, coarsely grated
1 x 215g tin of refried beans
1–2 tablespoons boiling water
a splash of olive oil
1 ripe avocado, sliced
300ml sour cream, some for the top and some in a serving bowl
20g coriander leaves
jalapeño peppers, from a jar (optional)
300–400g good quality fresh tomato salsa (from the chilled supermarket aisle), to serve

Heat the oil for the chilli in a frying pan over a medium–high heat. Add the onion and garlic and cook for 8–10 minutes, stirring frequently, until soft. Add the beef mince and break it up with your spoon. Allow the beef to brown and crisp a little by stirring and cooking it for 10–15 minutes. Add the tomato paste, chilli powder and water and stir the whole mixture together to coat the beef in the sauce. Season well with salt and pepper and cook for 5–6 minutes more. Remove from the heat and leave to one side.

Preheat the oven to 180°C/160°C fan/gas 4.

Spread an even layer of tortilla chips over a baking tray, covering the whole base of the tray. Sprinkle half the grated cheese over the tortilla chips, then add a second layer of tortilla chips. Spread the beef mixture evenly over this layer, then top with another layer of tortilla chips and the remaining cheese. Pop it in the oven to bake for 8–12 minutes, or until the cheese is bubbly and melted, and some of the exposed edges of the tortilla chips are golden brown.

Empty the tin of refried beans into a small saucepan and reheat over a medium–low heat, stirring frequently. Add a tablespoon or two of boiling water and the splash of olive oil to loosen it a little. The beans firm up quite quickly, so they're best eaten hot.

Remove your nachos from the oven and serve in a large bowl or on a platter, topped with the sliced avocado, dollops of sour cream, coriander and slices of jalapeño, if you like, with bowls of salsa, sour cream and refried beans for dipping. It's a bit messy, but so delicious!

Mum's tip

Don't save all your best plates and cutlery for the extra-special occasions, give them the love they deserve even at the more low-key get together!

If you aren't one to celebrate Christmas, then maybe New Year's Eve is at the top of your hosting list for the end of the year. It's a time that family or friends can get together to see in the new year with a flute of champagne and a dodgy party hat! It's about fresh starts, goal setting and go-getting and it usually comes with a few emotional attachments too. If you've had a terrible year that felt as though it was never ending, it's a time to accept it, bury it and look ahead to a new start.

If you've had the best year ever, it's also a time to celebrate that and hope for another year that will be just as great! It's also worth realising that on New Year's Eve you could be surrounded by people in either of those categories, so it's about making it special enough for both and ensuring that everyone has a good time. It's only right to start off the year in the best way possible.

HOSTING THE PARTY OR ORGANISING AN EVENT?

There are so many things going on at New Year that sometimes it's a little more appealing just to book tickets and go to a professional event being hosted in your nearest town or city, or in the local pub with free drinks and fireworks. Chat to your friends and family and see what kind of night they want. It might be that they'd prefer to go out, in which case you can set about finding the perfect evening for everyone and book it far in advance. If you decide to host though, read on!

SET A THEME

For a New Year's party, you can just about set any theme you want! If you want to do fancy dress and are stuck for ideas, you could ask guests to dress as something beginning with a certain letter or to dress as someone or something connected to an event that happened during the year. I really like this one as you can get quite creative and arrive as your favourite meme of the year, or be a celebrity acting out their shocking moment! (Not going to lie: creating the costume for Kim Kardashian's cover shoot for *Paper* would have been epic.) I also think a metallic theme works well for New Year – maybe you want your decorations to be holographic, gold or silver. Either way this can be included in every aspect – napkins, balloons, streamers, tablecloth and even the invites!

INVITATIONS

You can make these or have them designed online, printed and mailed to you. Or you can design them on the computer and email them to your guests, whichever you prefer. I personally like to have the physical thing, but then I think I'm a bit old-fashioned in that sense, as well as far too sentimental. Make sure to send these out well in advance (preferably a

TIP

Ask if anyone wants to make a speech. These are usually a lot more fun and sentimental when they're spontaneous (or after a few beverages) but make for a lovely end to an evening.

Mum's tip

Always say thank you after the event – even if just by text or WhatsApp. Or go that extra mile with a note card. Saying thank you means a lot.

couple of months at least), as New Year is the sort of time where everyone feels as though they need to make plans ahead of time so they aren't spending it doing nothing.

CREATE A PLAYLIST

Using music from the year you're saying goodbye to is always fun! As well as anything that could fit into your theme.

FOOD AND DRINK

I think for a party like this, it's better to have a more mezze/tapas-style food display that people can help themselves to. It's definitely always my go-to with larger groups as it feels a lot less daunting than preparing a starter, main and dessert while everyone waits around a huge table, although if you have a smaller number of people coming and formal dining is more your style, then go for it. Help-yourself means you are able to be a little more free when preparing the food, and you can keep topping it up or bringing new things out throughout the evening without that added pressure of making sure everything is done at the same time. (See my recipes for canapés on pages 226–233.) It's also the perfect time to make sure your bar cart or alcohol stash is fully stocked with everything that you need for a bit more of a boozy

party! You should also take into consideration that when people are drinking up until midnight, they are more likely to be a little more sozzled by the time the clock strikes twelve – so leave out a good selection of soft drinks too. (See over the page for bar cart inspiration!)

GAMES AND ENTERTAINMENT

As this will be a pretty lively party, you want to keep spirits high by planning some fun games that everyone can join in with. You can refer back to my games ideas on pages 216–217 to see which sort of games might be appropriate here. Another thing I always think brings heaps of entertainment is a photo booth or a photo shoot area! All this requires is a sheet of fabric or a backdrop set up against a wall, a few photo-booth props, a good light (a ring light would be ideal for this) and your mobile phone. You could even make the props yourself and tie them into the theme of the party, asking your guests to share their photos using a hashtag so you can all join in on the photo fun!

Since it's a New Year's Eve party, you may want some streamers, party poppers or fireworks to bring in the new year together, so think about what you're going to do for the countdown! It's one of those moments you don't want to forget, so you'll all need to congregate with enough time.

BAR
STYLING

Bar carts became very popular in many homes from the 1950s and have recently had a bit of a resurgence. It's essentially a hostess (or a party go-ers) dream. It can be a beautiful piece of décor in the corner of your room but also very functional and useful when it comes to hosting a party. I've had my bar cart for a few years now and, although I'm aware not everyone reading this section of the book will own a bar cart, it's more about creating a space that's both practical and nice to look at where you keep and store your alcohol, or how you choose to display it when you have guests over.

It doesn't need to be a place just for liquids, as it's also nice to consider things like a bucket of ice, a cocktail shaker and a cocktail set, which allows people to get a bit creative and have fun when creating their evening concoction (and sometimes a sticky floor...).

Another thing to consider is what you might want to garnish and dress your drinks with. You could leave out fruit like lemons and limes, herbs like mint and thyme and also slightly more tailored drink accompaniments like juniper berries, pink pepper or edible flowers/petals (see some of my cocktail recipes on pages 104–105).

If your bar cart or space is a more permanent fixture in your home as opposed to just being used at a party, it's nice to think about other elements you can add to allow it to become more than just a drinks cabinet. I have a neon sign on mine and often place a house plant on it to give it a bit more colour and character. I also think it's nice to display some fun glasses/cups and to have colourful paper straws for people to grab and go.

TIP

If you're serving champagne or prosecco, as well as the standard bevvies, think about the pretty things you can add to make it look incredible like candyfloss, sugared flowers or edible glitter!

CHEESE & HAM ARANCINI BITES

If you're not serving a full meal to your guests, it's still important that they don't go hungry. If you have alcohol at your party then it's even more important to feed people something a bit stodgy! It's best to make the risotto the day before so it has time to cool, and then finish off the arancini on the day. Don't make them any further in advance though as you should always use rice within 24 hours of cooking it.

PREP: 20 minutes
COOKING: 50-60 minutes
COOLING: at least 1 hour, but
    preferably overnight

MAKES 10

for the risotto mixture
a small knob of butter
1 tbsp olive oil
1 small onion, finely chopped
1 garlic clove, finely chopped
1 litre vegetable stock
a pinch of saffron strands
    (optional)
250g Arborio rice
75g Parmesan, grated, plus
    extra to serve
90g smoked ham, cut into thin,
    2cm-long batons (optional)
salt and black pepper

for rolling the arancini
100g plain flour
2 large eggs
200g fine dried breadcrumbs
1 litre vegetable oil

For your risotto mixture, allow the butter to melt with the oil in a heavy-based pan over a medium-high heat. Add the onion and cook for 5-6 minutes, stirring frequently, until beginning to soften. Add the garlic and cook for 4-5 minutes.

In the meantime, pour the stock into another saucepan and add the saffron, if using (it will make the risotto an amazing gold colour). Gently heat the stock over a medium-low heat and leave it to sit on the hob while you cook your risotto.

Once the onion and garlic are soft, add the rice. Stir together then add a ladleful of hot stock and stir to allow the rice to absorb the liquid. Once the first ladleful of stock has been almost fully absorbed, add a second, stirring as you go. Repeat this, allowing each addition of stock to be absorbed by the rice before adding the next. Taste the rice – if it is still hard at the centre, keep adding stock, but stop once the rice is almost completely soft. You might not need all the stock. This will take about 35-45 minutes. Stir through the Parmesan and season with salt and pepper. If you're using it, stir the ham through. Allow to cool completely, storing it in the fridge if you're not making the arancini until the next day. If you're in a hurry, tip the risotto out onto a baking tray or roasting dish to give it more surface area and speed the cooling.

To make your arancini, tip the flour into a shallow bowl, then break the eggs into a second bowl and beat them lightly. Put the breadcrumbs in a third bowl. Heat the vegetable oil in a deep, heavy-based pan over a high heat – it mustn't be more than a third full when the oil is in. Test the heat of the oil: when you sprinkle in a pinch of breadcrumbs, if the oil sizzles and bubbles around the floating crumbs, it's ready.

While the oil is heating, scoop up some cooled risotto mixture in your hands and roll into a 5cm ball. Dip it in the flour, then the beaten egg and finally roll it through the breadcrumbs, making sure the ball is completely coated in the crumbs. Set it on a plate and repeat with the rest of the risotto mixture.

Carefully lower the risotto balls into the hot oil with a slotted metal spoon, in batches of 4 or 5, depending on the size of your pan. Cook for 8-10 minutes, or until golden brown and crispy on all sides. Remove from the oil with the slotted spoon and place on a plate lined with kitchen paper. Turn the heat off under the pan of oil and allow it to cool completely before attempting to move it or discard the oil. Serve the arancini hot or at room temperature, sprinkled with a little more Parmesan over the top and maybe some mustard to dip if you like.

MINI VEGETABLE SAMOSAS

I am not usually a big fan of spicy food but these little veggie samosas have the perfect amount of heat and I think a little spice is good for a drinks party. The cooling yoghurt and mango dips are really refreshing too. See page 227 for photograph.

PREP: 35 minutes
COOKING: 1 hour 15 minutes

MAKES 21

1 tbsp vegetable oil
1 onion, finely chopped
2 garlic cloves, crushed
1½ tbsp curry powder (mild, medium or hot, your choice)
1 tsp ground turmeric
1 tsp ground cumin
2 potatoes, peeled and cut into 5mm–1cm cubes
1 carrot, peeled and cut into 5mm–1cm cubes
150g frozen peas
200ml vegetable stock
1 x 270g pack of filo pastry (7 sheets)
100g butter
50g sesame seeds
salt and black pepper

to serve
mango chutney
natural yoghurt

Heat the vegetable oil in a large frying pan over a medium-high heat and cook the onion and garlic for 8–10 minutes until the onion is soft and beginning to brown. Add your spices, season with salt and pepper and stir to coat the onion in the curry flavours.

Add the potatoes, carrot and peas to the pan. Pour over the vegetable stock, cover the pan, reduce the heat to low and cook for 30–40 minutes, or until the potato is soft but not mushy. Take off the heat and allow the mixture to cool completely.

Preheat the oven to 200°C/180°C fan/gas 6 and remove the filo pastry from the fridge to allow it to come up to room temperature. Line a baking tray with non-stick baking paper. Melt the butter in a small saucepan.

Unwrap the pastry and carefully separate out one sheet. Cover the rest of the sheets with a damp clean tea towel to prevent them from drying out while you work with the first one. Lay the single sheet, with a short edge facing you, on a clean, dry work surface and, using a sharp knife, cut it lengthways into 3 long, even strips.

Take a tablespoon of your cooled filling mixture and place it at the bottom edge of one of the strips of pastry. Brush the rest of the strip with a good layer of melted butter, making sure to get to the edges. Then bring the bottom right corner of the pastry up over the filling to make a triangle shape, enveloping the filling mixture. Fold this pocket up and over itself, then bring the bottom left corner up to meet the right vertical edge. Then fold it over itself again. Continue folding the triangle up the strip of pastry, to seal all the open edges. Brush the samosa with more melted butter to seal it all together, then place on the lined baking tray and scatter with sesame seeds. Continue folding the rest of the potato filling into the pastry strips to use up all the sheets of filo.

Bake your samosas in the preheated oven for 20–25 minutes, or until golden brown and crispy. Remove them from the oven and allow to cool on a wire rack. Serve warm with mango chutney and yoghurt for dipping.

BREADED MOZZARELLA

These are so delicious – like a grown-up version of cheese on toast. Make sure you use the blocks of mozzarella and not the balls as they won't cook properly. See page 230 for photograph.

PREP: 1 hour 15 minutes
COOKING: 10 minutes

MAKES about 20

100g plain flour
2 large eggs
2 tbsp milk
150g panko breadcrumbs
1 tsp dried basil
1 tsp dried oregano
1 tsp garlic powder (optional)
500g cooking mozzarella
  (see intro), cut into chunky
  batons
500g good quality tomato
  and basil pasta sauce,
  preferably organic (from
  a jar)
a pinch of dried chilli flakes
  (optional)
1 litre vegetable oil
salt and black pepper

Tip the flour into a shallow bowl, then break the eggs into a second bowl and beat them lightly with the milk. Put the panko breadcrumbs in a third bowl and add the herbs, garlic powder, if using, and some salt and pepper.

Coat each mozzarella baton in the flour, then dip in the milky egg, then roll it in the seasoned panko to coat completely, placing each baton on a greaseproof paper-lined baking tray while you make the rest. Once you've coated all the batons, place the tray in the freezer for 1 hour, to set the coating.

Heat the tomato sauce in a small pan over a medium heat, adding the chilli flakes if you'd like it a little spicy. If the sauce is quite chunky, blitz it to a smoother consistency with a hand blender. Keep it warm, transferring it to a bowl to serve when ready.

Heat the vegetable oil in a deep, heavy-based pan over a high heat – it mustn't be more than a third full when the oil is in, so choose a larger saucepan than you think you'll need. Test the heat of the oil: when you sprinkle in a pinch of breadcrumbs, if the oil sizzles and bubbles around the floating crumbs, it's ready.

Carefully lower the mozzarella batons into the hot oil using a slotted metal spoon and fry, in batches, for 2-3 minutes, until an even golden brown on all sides. Remove them carefully with the slotted spoon and place them on a plate lined with kitchen paper to blot away the extra oil. Sprinkle with a little salt while they're still hot. (Turn the heat off from under the pan of oil and allow it to cool completely before attempting to move or discard the oil.)

Serve the breaded mozzarella hot, with the tomato and basil sauce for dipping.

FIRECRACKER CHICKEN

These sweet and sticky skewers are perfect for evening nibbles or larger parties! See page 231 for photograph.

PREP: 15 minutes, plus
  2 hours marinating time
COOKING: 25 minutes

SERVES 8–10 as a nibble
  (or 2–3 as a main course)

3 boneless, skinless chicken
  breasts, cut into long strips
2 tbsp vegetable oil, plus a little
  extra for greasing
2 tbsp sesame seeds

for the marinade
2 shallots, finely chopped
3 garlic cloves, minced
1–2 Thai chillies, finely chopped
5cm piece of fresh ginger,
  peeled and finely chopped
2 tbsp dark soy sauce
2 tbsp light soy sauce
2 tbsp fish sauce
4 tbsp soft brown sugar

for the sauce
4 garlic cloves, grated
1–2 Thai chillies, finely chopped
2 tbsp sesame oil
3 tbsp white wine vinegar
4 tbsp honey
100g ketchup
4 tbsp soft brown sugar
120ml light soy sauce

essential equipment:
skewers

If you're using wooden skewers, soak them for 30 minutes before you use them, to ensure they don't burn.

Mix your marinade ingredients together in a bowl and stir well to dissolve the sugar. (You can also make this by blitzing the ingredients in a food processor to a paste.) Add the strips of chicken to the marinade and leave to marinate for at least 2 hours, but overnight would be best (in the fridge).

For your sauce, put the garlic and half the chillies in a pan. Add the remaining sauce ingredients and bring to a simmer over a medium heat. Allow to reduce, stirring frequently, for about 10 minutes, until it has thickened and darkened to a nice deep brown. Taste the sauce – if you'd like it spicier, add the rest of the chopped chilli. Keep warm.

Preheat the oven to 180°C/160°C fan/gas 4. Arrange a wire rack over a baking tray and brush it with a little vegetable oil.

Remove the strips of chicken from the marinade and thread them onto the skewers, weaving each piece back and forth up the sticks. Place on the wire rack over the baking tray and cook in the oven for 10 minutes, then turn them over, baste with a little bit of the marinade and cook for another 10 minutes, or until fully cooked through.

Serve the chicken hot on a platter, topped with the sesame seeds, and with a bowl of the warm sauce for dipping.

SALMON, PRAWN, AVOCADO & CUCUMBER TARTLETS

These delicate little bites add something light and fresh to a canapé selection. You can actually also buy mini tart cases and use those instead, which will make everything a lot easier! Make these last, just before your guests arrive, so that everything stays fresh. See page 230 for photograph.

PREP: 30 minutes
COOKING: 10–15 minutes
MAKES 10

1 sheet of ready-rolled
 all-butter puff pastry
1 large egg
1 tbsp milk

for the filling
100g cooked and peeled
 prawns, defrosted if frozen
100g smoked salmon,
 chopped into 1cm pieces
$1/2$ cucumber, peeled, halved
 lengthways, deseeded and
 cut into 1cm cubes
1 ripe avocado, cut into 1cm
 cubes
juice of 1 lemon
1–2 dashes of Tabasco
 (optional)
salt and black pepper
a few sprigs of dill, to serve

essential equipment:
5cm round, fluted pastry
 cutter
3cm round, plain pastry
 cutter

Take your pastry out of the fridge about 20 minutes before you start working with it (so that it doesn't crack). In a small bowl, beat the egg and milk together.

Preheat the oven to 200°C/180°C fan/gas 6 and line a baking tray with non-stick baking paper.

Unroll the pastry and leave it on its parchment backing paper on the work surface. Using a 5cm round, fluted pastry cutter, cut out 20 rounds of pastry. Arrange 10 of these on the lined baking tray. Take a 3cm round, plain pastry cutter and cut the centres out of the remaining 10 rounds to create rings. Discard the cut-out centres.

Brush the full rounds with a layer of egg wash, then top each with a ring. Brush the tops of the rings too. With a sharp, pointed knife, trace around the centre of each ring onto the round base, but not cutting all the way through it. This will help the pastry rise around the edges. Pop in the oven to cook for 10–15 minutes, or until the little tart cases are puffed up and golden brown. Remove from the oven and allow to cool on a wire rack.

For the filling, drain the prawns in a sieve to get rid of any extra water; shake them to be sure. Roughly chop into similar sized pieces as the smoked salmon. Add them to a bowl with the salmon. Add the diced cucumber and avocado to the bowl.

Pour the lemon juice over everything, then very gently toss it together with a spoon. Season well with salt and pepper and add a tiny drop of Tabasco, if you fancy a little spice. The acid in the lemon juice will prevent the avocado from going brown, so be sure that there is enough – add a little more, if you think it needs it.

Spoon about 1–2 teaspoons of your filling into each pastry case and top with a little pinch of fresh dill.

THE PERFECT CHEESEBOARD

In my opinion, a cheeseboard is non-negotiable around Christmas and New Year. These days, supermarkets do a huge range of really special cheeses, especially in the run-up to Christmas, so take advantage and buy some things you maybe haven't tried before. The only important thing to remember is to have a range of types and lots of fresh and tasty things to serve with it, as well as some really good biscuits!

PREP: 10 minutes, plus enough time for the cheeses to come up to room temperature

SERVES 10–12, with leftovers to nibble the next day

A balanced cheeseboard should have a hard cheese, a soft cheese, a blue cheese and a goat's or sheep's milk cheese, but there are no hard and fast rules. Remember to take your cheese, especially the soft varieties, out of the fridge well in advance of serving them.

Choose 4–6 from the following suggestions:
200–300g extra mature Cheddar – it's not really worth messing with the best English Cheddar

300g blue cheese – Stilton is a great choice, but there are others out there, like gorgonzola or Roquefort

1 whole Camembert, or a large wedge of Brie – French versions are delicious, but there are some equally delicious varieties from Cornwall and Somerset these days

200–300g nutty, smooth continental cheese, such as Comté, Gouda, pecorino or Manchego

1 whole soft, strong cheese, like Vacherin du Haut, Reblochon or Époisses – these sometimes come in their own box, which looks really special as part of a big board

200g goat's cheese – soft, hard or with a rind, it's a nice way to add some tanginess to the selection

200g something different – this is your chance to add some colour; try a Wensleydale with cranberries, Red Leicester or a smoked Cheddar

to serve
crusty baguette, sliced

biscuits for cheese – water biscuits, digestives, cream crackers, Cornish wafers, or fancier charcoal biscuits or sourdough crispbread

oatcakes

fresh fruit – apples, pears, figs, grapes of all colours

dried fruit – apricots, dates, dried figs

chutney, honey and quince paste – my homemade chutney on page 51 makes a delicious accompaniment, but piccalilli, red onion relish (see page 114) and chilli jam are also popular condiments for a cheeseboard. Honey is delicious when drizzled over saltier, hard cheeses. Quince paste works really well with cheeses like Manchego.

Don't forget the cheese knives and small spoons before serving your guests!

WEEKEND BRUNCH

I love making this easy, relaxed breakfast for friends – I've made it so many times for people they're beginning to expect it when they stay. It's simple ingredients but with a bit of effort on the presentation it can look really impressive!

PREP: 5 minutes
COOKING: 20–30
  minutes

SERVES 4

16 tomatoes on the vine
1 tbsp olive oil
4 large free-range eggs
4 thick slices of
  sourdough
butter, for spreading
2 avocados
sesame seeds
a small handful of cress
a few basil leaves
balsamic glaze (see page
  52 or buy some!)
paprika

Preheat your oven to 180°C/160°C fan/gas 4.

Place the tomatoes on a baking tray and drizzle with the olive oil. Cook for 20–30 minutes, or until they are nicely roasted and just starting to collapse.

Meanwhile, boil your eggs in a pan of water for 4½ minutes. Remove from the heat and place in a bowl of cold water. Carefully remove the shells in the bowl and keep until ready to serve.

Toast and butter the bread. Halve and slice the avocados.

When ready to serve, top each piece of bread with sliced avocado and an egg and serve with the tomatoes. Scatter with sesame seeds, cress and torn basil leaves. Finish with a dusting of paprika and drizzle balsamic glaze in circles around the edge of the plate for a more polished finish.

VALENTINE'S

———

Ahh Valentine's Day, that day of the year that splits the nation. There are the loved-up couples who go above and beyond to express their love for their partner by bringing huge bunches of roses home or booking an evening meal out in a fancy restaurant. Then there are the people who hate Valentine's Day and won't celebrate it at all, choosing instead to show their appreciation and love every day of the year. Then there are those who aren't in a relationship, don't want a relationship, or who are seeking one. Although Alfie and I do like to write each other a card every year and do something a little bit cute and meaningful, we don't go overboard. The idea of joining other couples in a restaurant where we're all celebrating the same thing doesn't really float my boat, but an opportunity to say 'I love you' is always welcome.

IF YOU'RE LOVED UP

If you are spending Valentine's Day with your partner you might want to think about something you can do together. Even something as simple as cooking dinner together, baking something or preparing a bit more of a special meal (the kind where you both sit at the dining room table, not in front of the TV). Run the other person a bath with their favourite bath products, or go for a romantic walk. I'm definitely more in the homemade, thoughtful and sentimental camp when it comes to occasions like this. Hand-written vouchers are also a really nice idea and you can personalise them, add a touch of humour and include things you know your partner would like.

IF YOU AREN'T

If the mere thought of Valentine's Day sends shivers down your spine, it might be better to throw a 'Palentine's' party! I absolutely love the idea of this. Friendships are just as important as romantic relationships and this gives us all the perfect excuse to turn Valentine's into something a bit different for everyone to enjoy. You could almost see it as a little mini hen-do, but for everyone! Or maybe just something for you and your BFF. Whoever you want to share it with, invite them round and celebrate everything you love about each other. Write cards, buy all the red love-heart decorations, get in all the snacks and pull out all your best chick flicks. It might also be really nice to ask your friends to bring any old photographs, diaries or love letters from old partners that you can all look at and laugh about. I did this recently with all my friends and we laughed until we cried! It was so much fun looking back at old memories and cringing at love letters that we received or wrote when we were teenagers.

Palentine's movie night suggestions

Mean Girls	*Now and Then*
Clueless	*My Girl*
Bring It On	*He's Just Not That*
Spice World	*into You*
Wild Child	*Bridesmaids*
The Greatest	*How To Lose a Guy in*
Showman	*10 Days*
Cruel Intentions	*500 Days of Summer*
10 Things I Hate	*The Devil Wears*
About You	*Prada*
Legally Blonde	*Dirty Dancing*
Miss Congeniality	*Never Been Kissed*
Titanic	*The Other Woman*
A Cinderella Story	*Crossroads*
The Notebook	

VALENTINE'S CUSHIONS

If, like me, you are sentimental in your gift giving or receiving, making something like this for your partner or best mate is a nice way of showing you love them!

For each cushion, you will need:

25cm square sheet of paper
pencil
fabric pins
pink or purple marl felt
– two 25cm squares and
one strip that is 80 x 5cm

red or white felt for the
lettering – 20 x 12cm
Bondaweb – 20 x 12cm
iron
pressing cloth or tea towel
sewing needles
matching sewing thread
approx. 25g polyester
fibrefill

Cutting out the hearts

1 Start by making a heart-shaped template. Fold the sheet of paper from corner to corner, then in pencil, draw half a heart along the fold. Cut out through both layers along the pencil line and open out. Pin the heart template on a square of coloured felt. Cut out one heart, then do the same with the second square of felt.

Adding the slogan

2 Print out your message in 3.5cm high letters using a plain font. (I have used Arial Rounded MT.) Cut out the letters and then turn them over, so they are the wrong way round.

3 Place the Bondaweb over the first letter, with the paper side facing upwards. Trace round the outside edge of your letter onto the paper side of the Bondaweb, using a pencil. Add the other letters, leaving a border of about 5mm around each one, then cut out each letter roughly.

4 Using a pressing cloth (or a tea towel) to protect the felt, iron the adhesive side of the Bondaweb letters onto the contrasting colour felt. Then cut out each letter along the pencil lines. Peel off the backing paper and arrange the letters on one felt heart (right way round), spelling out your message. Using a hot iron and the pressing cloth, press the letters to stick them in place.

Putting it all together

5 Cut a 5cm slit across the centre of the other felt heart. Fold the 80cm felt gusset strip in half and mark the centre with a pin. Match the centre top edge to the dip at the top of the heart, and pin the edge of the strip and the edge of the heart together, all the way around to the bottom point of the heart. Do the same on the other side of the heart, with the other end of the gusset strip, and fold back the spare felt where the two short ends meet up at the bottom point.

6 Now pin the heart with the slogan to the other edge of the gusset strip, making sure the letters are facing inwards. Roughly handstitch the hearts and gusset strip together along the pinned edges to hold it in place, then remove the pins. Machine stitch along the seams, 5mm from the edge, or sew by hand with back or running stitch. Over-sew the ends of the strip together by hand.

Stuffing the cushion

7 Turn the whole thing right side out by pushing the felt carefully through the 5cm slit. Ease out the seams and pad out the heart by stuffing the fibrefill through the small gap. Push the filling right into the top curves and bottom point to get a smooth shape.

8 Sew up the 5cm slit by hand and, if you want, disguise it by Bondawebbing an extra little felt heart over the seam.

SETTING THE TABLE

When it comes to hosting something a little more formal, setting the table is something you'd put a bit more thought and creativity into than you would for those more casual evenings where it's just you and your partner or a couple of friends. We don't often use our dining room unless there are more than six of us or it's a special occasion, but it definitely feels a lot more sophisticated and requires a bit more time and effort. That doesn't mean, however, that laying the table is particularly difficult or challenging or that you need a long list of items to make your dinner party function properly. Whenever I'd attend a fancy dinner or event I used to think recreating something as spectacular would be near enough impossible. Stunning tablecloths, napkins that look like swans, sixteen forks and knives that you have no idea what to use for, and centrepieces to rival a royal wedding. In reality, all you need is the idea, and you can run with it in whichever direction you want and according to what suits your table and your event, from casual dining to something more formal.

Deciding on a theme or a set-up that reflects your style and your dinner is where you start. If it's Christmas, you might want something a bit more glitzy, or perhaps a little more green and Scandinavian. Take repurposing into consideration or go for more of a mix-and-match style. I also think a lot about my dining room and what reflects the vibe and ties everything nicely to create the best atmosphere for guests.

I prefer to keep everything a bit more neutral and, as I love my marble table, it feels a shame to completely cover it, so a table runner going down the middle of the table is a preference in our house. It also adds a bit more dimension to the table and provides a place to put food dishes, jugs and condiments. The centrepiece is also worth thinking about: would you want to go down the wreath and large candle route, candelabras, little jars of flowers, or a mixture of all of them? As well as making it look beautiful, you'll also want to think practically about everything else you will need to fit on the table, or other things you might want to consider. Things like table confetti (which I especially love around Christmas time), tea lights, side plates, place mats, napkins, serving spoons, glasses and place names! Something that I think is just as important as having everything you need on the table is creating ambience with lighting and music. I tend to have the lighting a little bit lower and use candles and lanterns, as I feel this gives a much more relaxed environment, with a playlist on hand to reflect the theme or mood. Nobody will enjoy eating in bright white light with no music.

TIP

If you have a lot of new people coming to a dinner party, leave space on the place name cards for guests to write one interesting fact about themselves for others to see.

Mum's tip

Theme your dinner party by decorating your table accordingly (decorate your chairs too, if you can, with ribbon tied in a bow) and planning a menu that complements your theme.

ANTIPASTO SHARING PLATTER

Sharing food in the middle of the table always makes it feel much more special and intimate. Visit your local deli counter and stock up on a few of your favourite ingredients for this Mediterranean-style starter. Below are some suggestions – for me, the mozzarella burrata is a must though! The best thing about this dish is that once you've bought everything, it only takes a couple of minutes to arrange on the platter.

PREP: 10 minutes

Presentation

As this starter is all about appearances, make sure you use a nice wooden board, marble or slate slab or a large serving platter. You may also want to include a few smaller bowls for oily ingredients such as olives and sundried tomatoes. This can either be a sharing plate – where everyone eats directly from the central board – or you could provide small side plates so your guests can choose a few items at a time and place them on their own plate.

Build your plate by arranging the ingredients in a generous array. Gently fold the slices of cured meat, scatter vegetables around the board so everyone can reach some, drain the mozzarella, then tear it apart into big chunks and drizzle 1 tablespoon of the olive oil over it, to add some shine. Place slices of bread and/or crackers around the board.

This is a really adaptable dish – just add more ingredients if you are feeding a larger crowd.

Cured meats

Choose a few slices of a couple of different types of cured meat, e.g. prosciutto, salami, Parma ham, serrano or chorizo.

Cheeses

Ideally go for a contrast in texture and taste. Good suggestions include: buffalo mozzarella or burrata – or mini mozzarella balls, feta, strong cheddar, Comte and Manchego (also see The Perfect Cheeseboard on page 234).

Vegetables

For a fresher contrast choose a selection from: cherry tomatoes, olives, sundried tomatoes, roasted peppers or artichokes and a few rocket or other peppery salad leaves.

Bread

Focaccia, olive bread, baguette, cheese bread, breadsticks and crackers are all good additions. Instead of butter, dip your bread in the dressing below.

Dips and dressings

In a separate, shallow bowl, combine 1 tablespoon of balsamic vinegar with 2 tablespoons of olive oil – add them gently one at a time, and don't mix them, so that you can see a nice cloud of balsamic vinegar through the oil. This is a good dip for breads. Make sure you use a really good balsamic vinegar and olive oil here.

LADY AND THE TRAMP-STYLE SPAGHETTI & MEATBALLS

If you can find extra-long spaghetti, try recreating your own *Lady and the Tramp* moment! This recipe serves two, but you can easily double or quadruple the quantities. If you're serving fresh pasta rather than dried, allow 125g per serving.

PREP: 20 minutes
COOKING: 45–50 minutes

SERVES 2

180g dried spaghetti
garlic bread, to serve (optional)

for the meatballs
25g day-old bread, crusts removed
25ml milk
125g lean minced beef
125g minced pork
¼ onion, very finely chopped or grated
1 small garlic clove, crushed
½ tbsp finely chopped flat-leaf parsley
10g grated Parmesan, plus extra to
  serve
1 tsp salt
½ tsp black pepper
1–2 tbsp olive oil

for the sauce
1 tbsp olive oil
½ onion, finely chopped
1 garlic clove, finely chopped
340g passata
1 x 400g tin of chopped tomatoes
1 tbsp tomato paste
4 sun-dried tomatoes, finely chopped
1 tbsp dried oregano
1 tbsp balsamic vinegar
½ tbsp caster sugar
salt and black pepper

Tear the bread into chunks, then put into a shallow bowl with the milk. Set to one side to allow the bread to absorb the milk.

Put your beef and pork in a large mixing bowl and add the onion, garlic, parsley and Parmesan. Remove the bread from the milk onto your chopping board and mash it by finely chopping it with a knife. Add to the bowl with the remaining ingredients, apart from the oil, and mix it all together well using your hands.

Using clean hands, pinch out small clumps of meatball mixture, then roll between your palms to make even balls. (If you're aiming for perfection, 20g is a good size for each meatball.) Place your rolled meatballs on a baking sheet as you go and, if you aren't planning to cook them straight away, chill in the fridge until needed.

Heat 1 tbsp olive oil in a large, heavy-based frying pan over a medium–high heat. Add the meatballs to the pan, but don't crowd them in – if they don't all fit with space around each, cook them in batches (you may need a little more oil). Cook on all sides for 2–3 minutes per side to brown them, rolling them around the pan to get to all their edges (you're not looking to cook them through). Remove to a plate and set to one side.

For the sauce, add the oil to the same frying pan, over a medium–high heat. Cook the onion and garlic for a few minutes to allow the onion to soften slightly, then tip in the passata and tinned tomatoes and stir with a spoon to combine. Add the tomato paste, sun-dried tomatoes, oregano, vinegar and sugar to the pan. Season well with salt and pepper, stir the sauce, turn the heat to medium–low and let the sauce cook and thicken, uncovered, for 10 minutes, stirring occasionally.

Gently add your browned meatballs to the sauce. Turn the heat to low, cover the pan and let the meatballs cook in the sauce for 20 minutes or so.

Meanwhile, bring a large pan of salted water to the boil. Cook the pasta according to the packet instructions (for 8–12 minutes). Cook the garlic bread according to packet instructions, if using. Drain the pasta in a colander and remove the meatballs from the heat.

Make a nest of spaghetti topped with meatballs and a few spoonfuls of tomato sauce. Serve with the garlic bread. You can grate Parmesan over your own plate at the table.

CHOCOLATE PROFITEROLES

These look so pretty piled up on Valentine's Day. Instead of the usual cream filling, I've gone for a chocolate cream filling because we all deserve extra chocolate around this time of year!

PREP: 40 minutes
COOKING: 30–35 minutes
FILLING AND GLAZING:
  30 minutes
MAKES 12–15

for the choux pastry
100g plain flour
150ml water
50g unsalted butter, cut
  into cubes
2 tsp caster sugar
a pinch of salt
3 large eggs, beaten

for the chocolate filling
75g milk chocolate
  (preferably cooking
  chocolate), broken into
  chunks
200ml double cream

**for the white chocolate
  glaze**
100g white chocolate, finely
  chopped
1½ tbsp agave syrup (or
  golden syrup)
100ml double cream
1 tbsp caster sugar

to decorate (optional)
freeze-dried strawberries
fresh strawberries

essential equipment:
a piping bag fitted with a
  1.5cm–2cm plain nozzle
stand mixer or electric
  beaters

Preheat the oven to 170°C/150°C fan/gas 3½. Line a baking tray with non-stick baking paper. Sift your flour onto a separate sheet of baking paper, so it's ready to quickly tip into the pan in one go.

Put the water, butter, sugar and salt into a medium saucepan over a high heat and, once it has just reached boiling point, remove from the heat and chute the flour into the pan in one quick movement. Using a wooden spoon, quickly beat the mixture until it is completely smooth, which takes some vigorous arm action!

Return the pan to a medium heat and cook your dough for just 1 minute, beating the mixture until it dries a little bit and clumps together, almost cleaning the sides of the pan. Remove from the heat again and gradually add in the eggs, beating all the time, until you have a smooth dough. It will look strange and floppy for a while, but keep beating and it will come together. Spoon your warm dough into a large piping bag fitted with a large, 1.5–2cm, plain nozzle and let it cool and stiffen up a bit in the piping bag for about 5 minutes.

Using steady pressure, pipe 12–15 round choux buns onto the lined tray, about 4–5cm diameter. Allow plenty of space around each bun for them to grow in the oven. Wet your finger and, if the piping bag has left a pointed tip on the bun, gently push it down. Bake for 30–35 minutes or until golden, then transfer to a wire rack and use a skewer to poke a hole in the side of each, to allow the steam to escape. Set aside to cool completely.

For the filling, put the milk chocolate in a heatproof bowl and place the bowl over a pan of simmering water, making sure the bowl isn't touching the water. Stir occasionally until it is fully melted and smooth. Remove the bowl from the pan and allow the melted chocolate to cool to room temperature. Whip the cream in a bowl until it holds soft peaks, then gently fold the cooled, melted chocolate into the whipped cream. Chill in the fridge to firm up, then transfer the filling to a piping bag fitted with a large, plain nozzle.

Cut each choux bun horizontally in half with a small knife, pipe some filling onto the bottom half, then sandwich with the top, setting each one on a serving plate as you go, in a stack.

For the glaze, put the chopped white chocolate into a bowl. Add the syrup and set aside. Put the cream and sugar in a small pan over a medium heat. Gently heat, making sure you don't let it boil, stirring occasionally until the sugar dissolves, then pour it over the chopped chocolate. Allow it to sit and melt the chocolate for a few seconds before whisking until smooth and fully melted. Drizzle the glaze over the profiteroles just before serving. If you like, scatter over freeze-dried strawberries and serve fresh strawberries alongside.

DIRECTORY

———

To help you recreate some of the looks in *Cordially Invited* – or start your own collection of hosting essentials so that you have a stash on hand for the next time you plan an event – I have written down a few of my favourite places to grab decorations, homewares and stationery. There are endless places to source items from or find inspiration (both online and on the high street, catering for all different budgets, and locally to you) but these are my go-to places:

DECORATIONS & SUPPLIES

Party Pieces: partypieces.co.uk

Pretty Little Party Shop: prettylittlepartyshop.co.uk

Peach Blossom: peachblossom.co.uk

Amazon: amazon.co.uk

Ebay: ebay.co.uk

Lights4You: lights4you.co.uk

Etsy: etsy.com

Not on The High Street: notonthehighstreet.com

Funky Monkey Tents: funkymonkeytents.co.uk

HOMEWARES

Local Charity Shops

Anthropologie: anthropologie.com

Urban Outfitters: urbanoutfitters.com

Homesense: homesense.com/home

Igigi: igigigeneralstore.com/general-store

Oliver Bonas: oliverbonas.com

Next: next.co.uk/homeware

Asda / George Home: direct.asda.com/george/home-garden

Swoon: swooneditions.com

Made: made.com

West Elm: westelm.co.uk

H&M Home: hm.com

Zara Home: zarahome.com

Sainsburys Home: sainsburys.co.uk

John Lewis: johnlewis.com

Waitrose: waitrose.com

Marks & Spencer: marksandspencer.com

Ikea: ikea.com

Tesco: In-store homeware collections

Tiger: flyingtiger.com

La Redoute: laredoute.co.uk

Heals: heals.com

Houseology: houseology.com

CB2: cb2.com

Maisonsdumonde: maisonsdumonde.com

Habitat: habitat.co.uk

Trouva: trouva.com

STATIONERY

Paperchase: paperchase.co.uk

Rifle Paper Co: riflepaperco.com

INDEX

THANK YOUS

Putting this book together has been an absolute dream come true and there is no way it would be the book it is today if it wasn't for all these incredible and very creative people.

Firstly, my lovely team at Hodder who have taken my vision and done an amazing job at making sure the book reflected it down to the most minute detail. They have all been a joy and pleasure to work with: My favourite new person and Editor Briony Gowlett, Editor Laura Herring, Art Director Al Oliver, and Caitriona Horne and Eleni Lawrence in marketing and publicity.

My amazing team who have inspired and encouraged me in every aspect of creating this book and continue to be my biggest cheerleaders: Maddie, Carrie, Meghan, Danielle, Holly, Lauren, Sophie and Abigail. Thank you all so much for being such a driving force in this industry and in my life! They say behind every successful woman is a tribe of other successful women who have her back, and I am proud and very lucky to have you all alongside me (not behind me).

A huge thank you to the extremely talented and creative team who truly brought the book to life: My amazing photographer Susan Bell and her assistant Facundo, Designers Helen Crawford-White and Saffron Stocker, Props Stylist Louie Waller and her team Jade, Mischa and Sakara, food styling from Frankie Unsworth, Becks Wilkinson and Sophie Foot, Alex Heaton who worked with me to develop the recipes for the book, Lisa Pendreigh, Emily Dawe and Lucinda Ganderton who made our brilliant craft props for the photoshoot. Behind the scenes filmography from Duncan Smith, Hair Stylist Adam Cooke at Samantha Cusick London, Make-up by Eloise Parker and clothes styling by Hayley Lawrence.

To my friends and family – Mum, thank you for passing on your love of hosting, party planning and making people feel at home, I'm so glad you shared your very creative spirit with me. Dad, Joe, Amanda, Nick, Mark, Poppy, Sean, Tanya, Jim and Katie for all the support you have given me when putting this book together and being there on the shoot days! I appreciate and love you all.

Alfie, thank you for always being there for me when I need a bit of extra encouragement and making me believe in myself when I'm ever in doubt. Your support is what keeps me going!